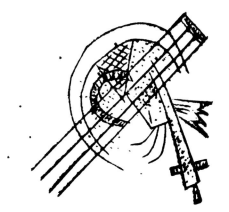

Hajo Düchting

WA**S** **KY**

MIDPOINT PRESS

FRONT COVER:
Detail from: *Yellow-Red-Blue*, 1925
Gelb-Rot-Blau
Oil on canvas, 127 x 200 cm
Paris, Musée National d'Art Moderne,
Centre Georges Pompidou

ILLUSTRATION PAGE 1:
Detail from: *Small Worlds X*, 1922
Kleine Welten X

ILLUSTRATION PAGE 2:
Small Worlds II, 1922
Kleine Welten II
Colour lithograph, four stones, 25.4 x 21.1 cm
Munich, Städtische Galerie im Lenbachhaus

BACK COVER
Kandinsky in his studio in Neuilly-sur-Seine, 1939
Photo: Paris, Musée National d'Art Moderne,
Centre Georges Pompidou

This edition published by Midpoint Press
by arrangement with TASCHEN GmbH

© 2001 TASCHEN GmbH
Hohenzollernring 53, D–50672 Köln
www.taschen.com
© 1993 for illustrations: A.D.A.G.P., Paris; VG Bild-Kunst, Bonn
Edited and produced by Christiane Heering-Labonté
Cover design: Catinka Keul, Angelika Taschen, Cologne
English translation: Ilmar Lehtpere

Printed in Germany
ISBN 3–8228–1547–0

Contents

Colourful Life, 1907
Das bunte Leben
Tempera on canvas, 130 x 162.5 cm
Munich, Städtische Galerie im
Lenbachhaus

him. The sensitive boy fled from these tensions into an inner world of mystery and fairy tale. The treasure of Russian as well as German fairy tales (read to him in German by his aunt) proved an enduring source for his artistic imagination. His first attempts to render these inner experiences into paintings were, however, in vain. The power of his experiences and his imagination exceeded by far his ability to present them in visual form. But the sensitivity of his aunt had awakened in him a love of art, which grew in spite of all the obstacles and detours on the way.

Kandinsky did not see his divorced parents as hostile figures of authority. They were merely two very different people who were devoted to him and who, in their own way, fostered his sensitivity. But particularly in his mother he saw the best qualities – "grave, austere beauty, well-bred simplicity, boundless energy," an ideal image of perfection, but also of tension and contrast, a picture he would emulate in theory and practice in his later years as a mature artist. In hindsight she appeared to him as the personification of "Mother Moscow"; Kandinsky believed that the source of his artistic endeavours lay in the combination of all his mother's contradictions and contrasts and the mental image of an "inner" Moscow. Kandinsky decided to study Law and Economics. Perhaps he chose these dry, academic fields of study to counterbalance his inner, unresolved tensions, or perhaps to flee from the troubling, unassimilated visions of his inner world. In 1886 he began his studies at Moscow University and so was again able to live in his beloved hometown. In his free time he continued to occupy himself with painting and Nature's "chorus of colour", which still confronted him with insoluble problems. Jurisprudence, which trained his sense for abstract relationships, was far easier. Economics fascinated him, as did the history of Russian Law and Peasant Law.

In 1889 a research assignment from the Society for Natural Science, Ethnography and Anthropology took Kandinsky to the province of Vologda, where he was to record the local peasant laws as well as the remains of the non-Christian religion of the original Syrian population. On this trip Kandinsky picked up abiding impressions of Russian peasant culture. The colourful decorative houses and furniture, the splendid folk costumes seemed like a magnificent painting to him. After this journey, whenever Kandinsky entered a Russian church or the countless Baroque chapels and churches in Bavaria, he felt as if he was in a picture. Subsequently Kandinsky saw this experience as another source of his artistic motivation: "to let the viewer stroll around within the picture, to force him to forget himself, and so to become part of the picture."

Sunday (Old Russian), 1904
Sonntag (Altrussisch)
Oil on canvas, 45 x 95 cm
Rotterdam, Museum
Boymans-van-Beuningen

"And suddenly for the first time I saw a picture. The catalogue told me it was a haystack. I could not recognize it as such. This inability to perceive was embarrassing. I felt that the painter had no right to paint so unclearly. Dully I felt that the subject of the painting was missing. And I noticed with astonishment and confusion that not only does the picture enthrall one, but also impresses itself indelibly on the memory, always quite unexpectedly appearing down to the last detail before one's eyes. This was all unclear to me and I was unable to draw any simple conclusions from this experience. But what was totally clear to me was the unsuspected power of the palette, a power which had earlier been hidden from me, but which surpassed all my dreams. Painting acquired a fairy tale strength and magnificence. And unconsciously the representational became discredited as an unavoidable element of a picture."   *Wassily Kandinsky*

The Society was so pleased with the results of Kandinsky's research that they made him a member. Little stood in the way of an academic career now, and Kandinsky continued to pursue this path, never seeming to waver at all. At the same time he became a member of the Law Society. In 1892 he passed his final law exams with ease and was given a lectureship at Moscow University. There he first noticed his cousin, Anya Chimiakin, the only female "observer" at the university at the time. He married her in 1892 after passing his exams, but their marriage remained more of a rational relationship based on friendship. Meanwhile his love of art, very much alive on a subliminal level, was rekindled by certain experiences, and once again Kandinsky was faced with the decision to choose either an academic career – including an offer of a professorship at Tartu University – or the insecure life of an artist. According to his own account, two events in particular had deeply moved him. One was the exhibition of French Impressionists in Moscow, at which Claude Monet's *Haystack* bewildered and amazed him. The second "shattering" experience that challenged his artistic sensibilities was seeing Wagner's *Lohengrin* at the Moscow Royal Theatre. The totally new orchestration of sounds stirred him deeply: "I saw all my colours in my mind's eye. Wild lines verging on the insane formed drawings before my very eyes." Music revealed the possibility of synaesthetic experience to Kandinsky and at the same time gave him a presentiment of the power of painting yet to be discovered. The relationship between colours and sounds, between music and painting, was not just theory to Kandinsky; it truly existed. This relationship gripped him to such a degree that the secret correspondence of the arts became a cornerstone of his artistic convictions, indeed the foundation of his painting.

All the tormenting uncertainty, the tensions he had quelled with his reason, broke out again. He only needed one more slight push to give in to the temptations of art, this time for good. As an academic with eclectic interests Kandinsky also followed the developments in other disciplines with unwavering keenness. The discovery of radioactivity by the French physicist Antoine Henri Becquerel in 1896 shook the foundations of the scientific conception of the world at that time – Kandinsky's included:

"In my soul the decay of the atom was the same as the decay of the whole world. Suddenly the sturdiest walls collapsed. Everything became uncertain, unsteady, and soft. It would not have amazed me, if a stone had melted into air before me and become invisible."

The academic road now seemed to him to be empty delusion, the research of scholars an accumulation of errors. Kandinsky's earlier artistic inclinations, his spiritual experience when preoccupied with artistic matters – these he had suppressed during his studies, but he had never given them up. Now they took on a totally different meaning. Art to him was no longer a means of confronting unbearable tension and disharmony, but rather the

The Singer, 1903
Die Sängerin
Coloured woodcut, three blocks in
secondstate, 19.5 x 14.5 cm
Munich, Städtische Galerie im
Lenbachhaus

exact opposite: it was the only way to adopt a more far-sighted position in this world of contradictions and inconsistency.

Kandinsky's decision was final; in 1896 he and his young
wife left Moscow. She was very reluctant to leave and uneasy
about facing the future at the side of an artist. Kandinsky went to
Munich to follow his vision of the new art.

Metamorphosis: Kandinsky in Munich 1896–1911

Kandinsky's decision in 1896, at the age of thirty, to study art in Munich was by no means a rash one. At that time Munich was considered a cosmopolitan city of art where such famous personalities as Franz von Lenbach or Franz von Stuck set the tone in the art world. In addition to this the "Munich Sezession" was founded in 1892, stirring up the ossified fronts between the naturalism of the Munich School, academic historicism and the advocates of symbolism. The "Sezession" included a host of artists following different lines, but among them were some of the most prominent art personalities of the time, painters such as Lovis Corinth, Adolf Hoelzel, Max Liebermann, Franz von Stuck, Hans Thoma, Wilhelm Trübner and Fritz von Uhde. Within a few years this group drew other secessions along in its wake, for example in Berlin and Vienna.

In the same year the journal *Jugend* was founded and in Germany Art Nouveau was accordingly known as Jugendstil. August Endell, a young architect, created an artistic scandal in that year with his plans for the Elvira Studio. He summarized the central idea of the new art in a pamphlet he published in 1896: "The greatest mistake one can make is to believe that Art is the precise reproduction of Nature." This revolutionary approach alluded primarily to the works of the sculptor Hermann Obrist, who caused a sensation with his bold abstract carpet designs, drawings and sculptures, and who a short time later, being an enthusiastic advocate of Jugendstil, founded the "Vereinigte Werkstätten für Kunst im Handwerk" (United Workshops for Art in Craft). Both Obrist and his pupil Endell had a direct influence on Kandinsky with their expressive use of colour and line.

But first of all Kandinsky underwent the strict discipline of drawing nudes at Anton Azbè's Art School, which he attended for two years without producing any work of note. Although he hated anatomical drawing, he tried to pick up the basics within a short time. Azbè's painting lessons were, however, far more important to him. Azbè painted in an Impressionist style and so stimulated Kandinsky to use a divisionist technique, using unmixed colours in juxtaposition, a style he later used in his small impressive landscape studies, for example *Beach Baskets in Holland* (p. 15), which is painted in thick patches of paint casually applied next to each other. One already notices the desire to be in sole command

Two Birds, 1907
Zwei Vögel
Woodcut, 13.6 x 14.4 cm

*Munich-Schwabing
with the church of St. Ursula*, 1908
München-Schwabing mit Ursulakirche
Oil on cardboard, 68.8 x 49 cm
Munich, Städtische Galerie im
Lenbachhaus

of visual elements, but they are not strictly systematic (as in post-Impressionist painting) and they are still far removed from Kandinsky's own abstract visual expression.

The anatomy classes with Professor Louis Moilliet, lively and stimulating as they may have been, did not give Kandinsky any appreciable inspiration or insight either. In fact, the suspicion grew in him that anatomy and art were two fundamentally different matters. "When some of my fellow students looked at my homework, they labelled me a 'colourist'. Some, not without malice, called me the 'landscape painter'. Both hurt me, although I could see that both descriptions were just. I really felt far more at home in the world of colour than the world of drawing. And I didn't know how I should confront the problem facing me."

After Azbè's lessons he confronted it by seeking out Franz von Stuck, regarded at the time as the best draughtsman in Germany. However, Stuck turned him away, telling him to take a drawing course at the Academy. Then came Kandinsky's next disappointment – he failed the entrance examination. He tried Stuck again and this time Stuck accepted him in his painting class, where Paul Klee and Hans Purrmann were also studying. Stuck was held in high regard both as a painter and as a teacher, and Kandinsky noted that Stuck taught him how to carry out the composition of a motif.

A year later Kandinsky left Stuck's studio to get on with his artistic development by himself. He had the support of like-minded fellow artists; at Azbè's he had already met Alexis von Jawlensky and Marianne von Werefkin, two Russian compatriots who had studied in Paris and were very familiar with the latest developments in French painting.

Old Town II, 1902
Alte Stadt II
Oil on canvas, 52 x 78.5 cm
Paris, Musée National d'Art Moderne,
Centre Georges Pompidou

Kandinsky also knew Ernst Stern, Stuck's studio assistant. Stern had perhaps already brought Kandinsky into contact with the puppeteer Waldemar Hecker and the sculptor Wilhelm Hüsgen. In any case, while Hecker, Hüsgen and Stern were involved in establishing "Die Elf Scharfrichter", the famous literary and artistic cabaret, Kandinsky was also looking for a group of artists with whom he could put a progressive exhibition programme independent of the academic scene into practice. In 1901 he founded "Phalanx", an association for artists and the exhibition of their work. He opened with an exhibition of his own work as well as the work of Alexander von Salzmann, a fellow student from Stuck's class, and work by his friends from the cabaret. To advertise the exhibition, Kandinsky designed a poster (p. 17) which transposed the stormy, progressive spirit of the association into subtle Jugendstil pictorial form. The progressive forces of the cultural scene in Munich gathered at the cabaret. Among them was Frank Wedekind, the dramatist. This intellectual climate provided Kandinsky with important stimuli, for he began to publish art criticism in Russian journals, in addition to producing paintings

Beach Baskets in Holland, 1904
Strandkörbe in Holland
Oil on canvas cardboard, 24 x 32.6 cm
Munich, Städtische Galerie im
Lenbachhaus

and graphics. But Kandinsky nevertheless found the art scene in Munich too conservative, too bourgeois and narrow-minded, dominated by doctrines of academic mediocrity. In the following "Phalanx" exhibitions he tried to present trends in art that he regarded as under-represented. These were mainly the work of Impressionist, Symbolist and Jugendstil (Art Nouveau) artists.

The second "Phalanx" exhibition was devoted mainly to Jugendstil works. Kandinsky himself felt more and more drawn to the potential of abstract forms in Jugendstil, and in his sketch books he drew many designs for appliqué, jewellery, ceramics and furniture.

However, he produced almost no large oil paintings in this initial period of experiment, devoting his time to the politics of the art scene. One of the earliest *Old Town II* (p. 14), shows a colourful view of a highly stylized town inspired by a trip to Rothenburg ob der Tauber. It perfectly expresses the fantastic unworldly mood that Kandinsky was caught up in in his early years in Munich. *The Blue Rider*, a painting that seems like a harbinger of what was to come, also belongs to this romantic genre of transfiguration.

The woodcut provided him with an adequate means of creating stylized forms and at the same time giving them a symbolic dimension. One of his earliest is the *The Singer* (1903; p. 11) which, with its flowing Jugendstil lines and ornamental division of space, has an obvious affinity to music. Kandinsky was convinced that there was an inner correspondence between a work of art and the viewer. He called this correspondence "Klang" (sound or resonance). *The Singer* could be an early expression of this belief, which Kandinsky later illustrated with a similar image in his theoretical work "Concerning the Spiritual in Art":

"Generally speaking, colour is a power which directly influences the soul. Colour is the keyboard, the eyes are the hammers, the soul is the piano with the strings. The artist is the hand which plays, touching one key or another, to cause vibrations in the soul."

In 1904 Kandinsky brought out a series of woodcuts entitled *Poems without Words*. He published a second series under the suggestive title *Xylographs* (xylograph is another word for woodcut but is also reminiscent of the word xylophone). In 1913 Kandinsky's last series of woodcuts appeared in *Klänge (Sounds)*, a book of poems and woodcuts. It was the climax of his work using this technique, a technique he regarded as most closely corresponding to lyrical poetry. The idea of merging the various art forms suggested by the synthesis of word, picture and sound in Kandinsky's woodcut cycles was common in all progressive circles in Munich and elsewhere, and accelerated the development of abstract visual expression.

The motifs of his woodcuts stemmed primarily from the world of folk tale and legend or Kandinsky's own imagination, which was particularly inspired by images from historical periods

Detail from the *Poster for the First Phalanx Exhibition*, 1901
Colour lithograph, 52 x 67 cm
Munich, Städtische Galerie im Lenbachhaus

Illustration opposite:
Cemetery and Vicarage in Kochel, 1909
Friedhof und Pfarrhaus in Kochel
Oil on cardboard, 44.4 x 32.7 cm
Munich, Städtische Galerie im Lenbachhaus

Illustration p. 18:
Gabriele Münter Painting in Kallmünz, 1903
Gabriele Münter beim Malen in Kallmünz
Oil on canvas, 58.5 x 58.5 cm
Munich, Städtische Galerie im Lenbachhaus

Illustration p. 19:
Gabriele Münter, 1905
Oil on canvas, 45 x 45 cm
Munich, Städtische Galerie im Lenbachhaus

such as the Middle Ages or the early 19th century Biedermeier. These mythical worlds facilitated the free use of colour and form and a gradual emancipation from the object. The woodcuts were Kandinsky's first step towards artistic independence. In these works he tried to realize his ideas and concepts for the first time. Some of Kandinsky's important paintings with romantic, fairy-tale themes, such as the oil painting *Couple Riding* (p. 6), profited from the technique, style and lyricism of his woodcuts. Against the dark background often found in this series small, colourful dabs of paint sparkle like gems. The setting is a riverside city, with cupolas very reminiscent of old Moscow. A couple, embracing, are riding through the unreal landscape. One is reminded of Kandinsky's description of "his" city, his undying love for "Mother Moscow", as well as of contemporary Jugendstil illustrations that served as a stimulus for his woodcuts. The ornamental structure of the composition and the simplified, stylized representation of objects are also related to art nouveau works. The colourful effect is stunning and again demonstrates Kandinsky's preoccupation with strong colourful impressions and their relation to mood. This use of colour also appears in the landscape studies in thick, glowing dabs of paint. But there they are bound up in the landscape, whereas in *Couple Riding* they seem to float freely and therefore stress the unreal overall mood, one far removed from the everyday scene.

The large tempera painting *Colourful Life* (p. 8), one of Kandinsky's most important works of this period, is also bound up in this mythical, transfigured Russian homeland. At first glance it appears to be a conglomeration of colourful figures moving aimlessly through an autumn landscape, with a magnificent city rising above it in solitary splendour at the top of a mountain. Gradually groupings of motifs and directions of movement become apparent and one begins to realize why Kandinsky called so few of his works a "composition", the highest possible accolade he could give a work of art. The painting is meant to depict all the worldly and spiritual aspects of Russian life past and present, aspects that touch upon death and the belief in resurrection, as well as strife and the small joys of everyday life. These themes can be found in altered form in Kandinsky's later work as well.

The free arrangement of the figures in the painting, the even surface texture and the light strokes of colour (partly divorced from representational functions) suggest Kandinsky's determination to move towards abstraction. In this and similar Russian scenes we see his efforts to bring out the typical and fundamental in his motifs, as well as to stress these qualities by means of his assertive use of form and colour. However, in spite of his continuing and intensive involvement in organizing exhibitions with the "Phalanx" group, Kandinsky did not manage to arouse the necessary interest in what he was doing. The work of both well-known and unknown Jugendstil, Symbolist and late Impressionist artists was exhibited by Kandinsky in the twelve "Phalanx" exhibi-

Interior (My Dining Room), 1909
Interieur (Mein Eßzimmer)
Oil on cardboard, 50 x 65 cm
Munich, Städtische Galerie im
Lenbachhaus

tions up until the dissolution of the group at the end of 1904. Particularly noteworthy were the exhibitions of work by Akseli Gallén-Kallela, a Finnish Symbolist, who produced decorative pictures inspired by Finnish legends, and Carl Strathmann, a painter and craftsman, whose expressive, ornamental style was another step towards the completely abstract pictorial conception that Kandinsky had in mind. Other high points were the exhibitions of work by Impressionist and post-Impressionist masters such as Claude Monet in the seventh exhibition in 1903, and Paul Signac, Theo van Rysselberghe, Felix Vallotton, Henri de Toulouse-Lautrec and other French painters of the time in the tenth exhibition in 1904. Apart from the praise and gratitude of a few close friends on the art scene, among them such important personalities as Peter Behrens, a member of the Darmstadt Artists Colony, Kandinsky earned nothing but abuse or hostile silence for these exhibitions, which were quite daring by the standards of the Munich art scene.

Grüngasse in Murnau, 1909
Oil on cardboard, 33 x 44.6 cm
Munich, Städtische Galerie im
Lenbachhaus

When the art school which was associated with "Phalanx"
proved to be unproductive as well, Kandinsky decided as president to dissolve the association. He turned down Behrens's offer
of a teaching post at the newly founded School of Arts and Crafts
in Düsseldorf. Trying to overcome his disappointment with the
Munich art scene, which had treated him with nothing but resistance and derision, he devoted himself to his woodcuts. His ideas
coincided most nearly and encouragingly with those of Jugendstil
and Symbolism. These movements showed him the possibilities
of the free, lyrical use of visual elements. Four friendships arose
from the ruins of "Phalanx". One of them was with Alfred Kubin,
whose work Kandinsky had presented in 1904 in the ninth exhibition. Kubin's demonic images and the virtuosity of his draughts-
manship fascinated Kandinsky. Through Kubin he met the Symbolist poets Stefan George and Karl Wolfskehl, with whom he
soon formed deep friendships. Perhaps Kandinsky recognized the
endeavours of kindred spirits in the mysterious, elitist poetry of
this circle – the attempt to found a new order in art on the basis
of a completely new premise that he for his part still had to estab-

lish in painting. He also formed a very close relationship with Gabriele Münter, a painter from Munich and his former pupil from the "Phalanx" period. Kandinsky and Münter lived and worked together after he and his wife had separated in Munich by mutual agreement (their goals and inclinations had been too incompatible, but after their separation they remained friends for years). Kandinsky found a sensitive, if difficult, partner in Gabriele Münter, who voiced her approval and criticism in the decisive years of his artistic breakthrough.

In the beginning the two artists travelled widely through Europe and back to Russia. During this time they spent a year in Sèvres near Paris, from June 1906 to June 1907. There Kandinsky worked on the woodcuts that he brought out in Paris in a portfolio entitled *Xylographs* in 1909.

He also exhibited his work in Paris in the avant-garde "Salon d'Automne" and the "Salon des Indépendants". There he met the Fauvist and Cubist artists. In the spring of 1908 Kandinsky and Münter returned to Bavaria. After years of unsettled life in the big cities of Europe and Russia, he again found peace and stability in

Murnau-View with Railway and Castle, 1909
Murnau-Aussicht mit Eisenbahn und Schloss
Oil on cardboard, 36 x 49 cm
Munich, Städtische Galerie im Lenbachhaus

Study for "Composition II", 1910
Studie zu "Komposition II"
Oil on canvas, 97.5 x 130.5 cm
New York, The Solomon
R. Guggenheim Museum

Murnau, a small town in the foothills of the Alps. From Munich, where they had finally settled down, they returned again and again to Murnau to paint. In 1909 they bought a house in Murnau and Kandinsky worked out the decorative interior design. He had again found a foothold; the landscape inspired him to new artistic efforts in which he sought to transfer his woodcut style to his landscape studies in oils. *Murnau-View with Railway and Castle* (p. 23) displays many of the characteristics of Kandinsky's woodcuts in its composition, particularly in the silhouetted flatness of the forms. The strong, thickly applied colours, in sharp contrast to the black of the train, were a new means of artistic expression. In other paintings as well, for example *Grüngasse in Murnau* (p. 22) or *Cemetery and Vicarage in Kochel* (p. 16), Kandinsky's new stylistic intentions are evident. They were surely also fuelled by the work of the Fauves and Nabis, which he had seen in Paris.

Kandinsky's paintings in this Murnau period are mostly composed of large solid areas of pure, bright colour set in sharp contrasts of light and dark or warm and cold. The paint is usually applied in thick dabs which are only occasionally detached from each other to let the ground colour show through. Areas of evenly applied colour often alternate with concentrations of different coloured dabs and blobs of paint, giving the paintings a restless, loud, flickering quality. Kandinsky takes his colours to extremes of tone and contrast. Representational themes have almost disappeared in the burgeoning flood of colour. Kandinsky's work is original in form and colour, even if some of his paintings, such as *Interior (My Dining-Room)* (p. 21), have elements in common with the Fauvist paintings of Matisse.

Kandinsky dispensed almost completely with the fairy-tale themes of his tempera pictures; only a few echoes of these found their way into works of this period, some of them enigmatic. Among these is *Picture with Archer* (p. 31). A knightly figure on horseback can be found in some of his paintings from this early period, for example in *Der Blaue Reiter*, and especially in his woodcuts. The fairy-tale motif developed more and more into a symbol of struggle and advance in Kandinsky's iconography, totally in keeping with the original meaning of "avant-garde" (i.e., "vanguard"). In *Lyrical* (p. 32) the horse and rider even take on monumental proportions, with the landscape receding into the background. In his final incarnation, the fairy-tale knight appears as Saint George, the dragon slayer, in many paintings, watercolours, woodcuts, sketches and verre églomisé pictures. The battling knight ultimately adorned the cover of *Der Blaue Reiter* almanac (cf. pp. 26 and 37).

During this period Kandinsky again found himself fighting for recognition. He invested his newly gained self-confidence in

Glass Painting with Sun, 1910
Glasbild mit Sonne
Verre églomisé, 30.6 x 40.3 cm
Munich, Städtische Galerie im
Lenbachhaus

Final draft for the cover of the *Blaue Reiter* almanac, 1911
Indian ink and watercolour over tracing and pencil, 27.9 x 21.9 cm
Munich, Städtische Galerie im Lenbachhaus

Illustration opposite:
Improvisation 6 (African), 1909
Improvisation 6 (Afrikanisches)
Oil on canvas, 107 x 99.5 cm
Munich, Städtische Galerie im Lenbachhaus

Illustration p. 28:
Mountain, 1909
Berg
Oil on canvas, 109 x 109 cm
Munich, Städtische Galerie im Lenbachhaus

Illustration p. 29:
Church in Murnau, 1910
Kirche in Murnau
Oil on cardboard, 64.7 x 50.2 cm
Munich, Städtische Galerie im Lenbachhaus

many plans and projects, starting work on a manuscript about his conceptions of art, arranging his sketches into veritable operas of colour, and again writing art criticism for Russian journals. The stimulating conversations in the Werefkin salon in Giselastrasse resulted in the formation of the New Society of Munich Artists in January 1909. As a driving force behind the organization, Kandinsky signalled his return to the Munich art scene. Members of the Society included Adolf Erbslöh, Alexander Kanoldt, Paul Baum, Vladimir von Bechtejeff, Erma Bossi, Karl Hofer, Moissey Kogan, the dancer Alexander Sacharoff and the art historians Heinrich Schnabel and Oskar Wittenstein, as well as Kandinsky's friends Münter, Jawlensky, Werefkin and Kubin.

Wilhelm Worringer's "Abstraction and Sensitivity" (1907) had reinforced Kandinsky's conviction that representational motifs were not necessary in art. Everywhere he looked he saw and gathered evidence of this new conception of art. He found ideas in Bavarian verre églomisé pictures and votive folk pictures, and made some verre églomisé pictures himself using free expressive forms (p. 25) which suppressed rather than stressed the representational. For a time he also pursued occult theories and devoted himself to the writings of Rudolf Steiner and Madame Helena Petrovna Blavatsky, the founder of the Theosophical Society. He was particularly interested in contemporary music and theatre. After a Schönberg concert he started a detailed correspondence with the originator of twelve tone composition about the relationship between music and art. He also found ideas for his operas of colour "The Yellow Sound" and "Violet Curtain" in the "Munich Artists' Theatre".

In spite of this intense examination of the intellectual trends of his time, Kandinsky still found time to organize exhibitions for the Society. It was not until the second exhibition (in autumn 1910) that he brought together an international collection of work by important modern artists such as Georges Braque, David and Vladimir Burliuk, André Derain, Kees van Dongen, Henri Le Fauconnier, Pablo Picasso, Georges Rouault and Maurice de Vlaminck.

Almost against the will of the city's sleepy, conservative art scene, Munich became a centre of avant-garde art. Kandinsky exhibited four of his own paintings and six woodcuts in the 1910 exhibition. *Composition II*, which was lost in the Second World War, was the largest and most important picture that Kandinsky had painted until then. It was characterized by liberation from perspective and the free use of line and colour in contrapuntal arrangement. Kandinsky still didn't dare take the plunge into the totally abstract. In *Study for Composition II* we can still recognize groups of figures, landscapes, houses, and again the horse and rider. But they are all in a state of diffusion, dynamically imbalanced, perhaps as a reflection of Kandinsky's mental state shortly before taking the plunge. The reaction of Munich's art critics was harsh, and they agreed unanimously that this painting was the

work of a madman or "someone under the effects of morphine or hashish". Only two voices were raised in favour of the exhibition – those of Hugo von Tschudi, the dedicated director of the Bayerische Staatsgemäldesammlungen, and Franz Marc, the still unknown Munich artist, who in his animal pictures was also seeking the essence beneath appearances and who would soon move toward colour-based abstraction in his painting.

As a result, Marc came into close contact with the Society, which accepted him as a member and elected him as their third president. At the beginning of 1911 Marc visited Kandinsky in Murnau and a deep friendship developed between them.

"The next morning I walked over to Kandinsky's. The hours spent with him are among my most memorable experiences. He showed me a lot of his older, as well as his latest things. The latest are all incredibly strong. At first I felt the great joy of his strong, pure, fiery colours, and then my mind began to work. You can't get these pictures out of your mind."

In 1909 Kandinsky began to divide his work into three categories – "Impressions", which still had an element of naturalistic representation; "Improvisations", which were supposed to convey spontaneous emotional reactions; and "Compositions", the highest and most complicated level, which could only succeed after a long period of preliminary work. But Kandinsky did not keep to the strict division of the categories. The classification of his pictures into these groups often seemed arbitrary. The titles "Improvisation" and "Composition" are yet another allusion to music. In the analogy of art and music Kandinsky saw his colours and forms "sounding" and "vibrating".

In *Improvisation 6* (*African*) (p. 27), the action suggested by two "African" figures is almost drowned by the colours that course through the picture in a bright, passionate tide of contrasts. Even if some pictures still have representational titles, such as *Mountain* (p. 28) or *Church in Murnau* (p. 29), all of Kandinsky's paintings from this period have an inner coherence in a careful step-by-step discovery of a new, independent language of colour and form. *Improvisation 19* (pp. 34–35) demonstrates perhaps best of all how far Kandinsky had ventured forward. Most of the space is occupied by modulations of blue, ranging from the lightest white-blue through purplish tones to dark ultramarine. This vibrant field of colour is framed by the shapes of the figures formed by black strokes on a foundation of strong warm colours on the left, and rising on the right almost to the edge of the picture over a ground of blue. Although the black outlines still suggest the figurative, there is absolutely no connection between the two groups of figures and any recognizably representational content in the rest of the picture. Perhaps Kandinsky found inspiration for this work in the performances of the "Munich Artists' Theatre", which presented its Symbolist pieces against a two-dimensional pictorial backdrop. In 1914 Hugo Ball suggested a performance of Kandinsky's stage composition "The Yellow

Picture with Archer, 1909
Bild mit Bogenschützen
Oil on canvas, 177 x 147 cm
New York, The Museum of Modern Art
Fractional gift of Mrs. Bertram Smith

Sound" at this theatre, but it never came off. Some scenes from this opera of colour are reminiscent of the shapes of colour in *Improvisation 19*.

Kandinsky's fellow artists in the Society found these developments completely alien, and criticism of these paintings mounted. When exhibitions were actually cancelled because of this, tensions rose in the organization, leading to Kandinsky's resignation as president. Erbslöh and Kanoldt took the helm. They both tended towards a measured form of Cubism. Marc and Kandinsky saw the break coming and in the summer of 1911 made plans for new directions in art, to be published in book form under the title "Der Blaue Reiter". The situation between the conservative and progressive artists' circles worsened when Carl Vinnen, a Worpswede artist, published a pamphlet expressing the general disquiet felt by conservative German artists' over the influence of foreign (i.e., French and Russian) art. At the instigation of Franz Marc an answer was immediately published by Piper, a Munich publishing house, containing statements by Marc and Kandinsky as well as other artists, writers and museum directors. Kandinsky's commit-

Lyrical, 1911
Lyrisches
Oil on canvas, 94 x 130 cm
Rotterdam, Museum Boymans-van Beuningen

Romantic Landscape, 1911
Romantische Landschaft
Oil on canvas, 94.3 x 129 cm
Munich, Städtische Galerie im
Lenbachhaus

ment to this issue was also viewed with increasing distrust by his Society.

The final row came in December 1911, when the jury for the third Society exhibition turned down Kandinsky's *Composition V* on the grounds that its size was not in accordance with Society rules. Marc and Kandinsky immediately resigned and were followed by Münter and Kubin. As a result the authority and innovative power of the group was broken, a fact that even the publication of a book entitled "Das neue Bild" (i.e., "The New Picture") could not change. Kandinsky's old companion, the painter Marianne von Werefkin, expressed her indignation at the group's lack of understanding for Kandinsky's goals. She and Jawlensky also resigned in 1912 and the Society ceased to exist.

Improvisation 19, 1911
Improvisation 19
Oil on canvas, 120 x 141.5 cm
Munich, Städtische Galerie im
Lenbachhaus

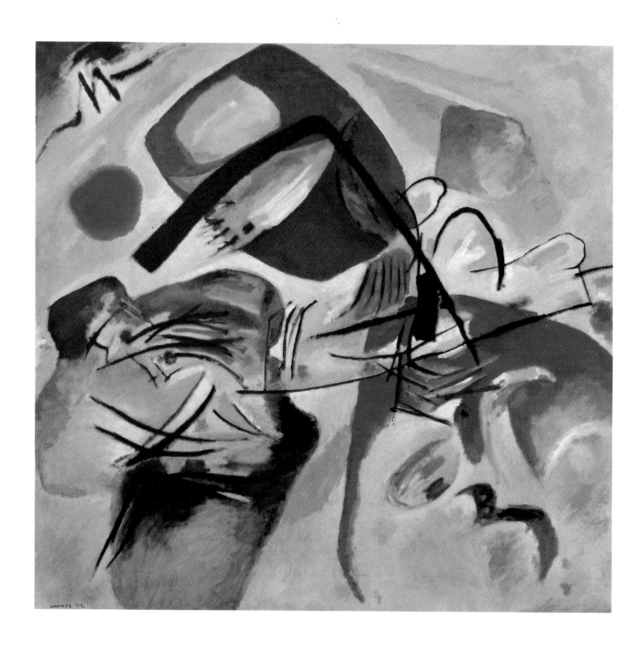

Breakthrough to the Abstract:
"Der Blaue Reiter"
1911–1914

The legendary first exhibition of "Der Blaue Reiter" opened in the room next to the third Society exhibition at the Moderne Galerie Thannhauser on 18 December 1911. Kandinsky was represented by work from all three of his categories: *Impression-Moscow*, *Improvisation 22* and the controversial *Composition V*, which had caused such a scandal. The other artists in the show included Marc, Macke, Münter, Schönberg, Henri Rousseau, the brothers David and Vladimir Burliuk, Heinrich Campendonk, Robert Delaunay, Eugen von Kahler, Elisabeth Epstein, Jean Bloé Niestlé and Albert Bloch. The small catalogue also announced the publication of the *Blaue Reiter* almanac, which Kandinsky and Marc had been working on for some time.

In the foreword to the catalogue Kandinsky tried to prepare visitors for the rather heterogeneous composition of the exhibition. "We are not seeking to propagate any precise or special form in this small exhibition. Our purpose is to show, in the variety of the forms here represented, how the inner wish of the artist takes shape in manifold forms."

The exhibition did indeed offer stunned visitors a somewhat baffling picture of new art. One could easily identify with the virtuoso bird paintings of Niestlé, a friend of Franz Marc. But hanging next to them were the unearthly visions of Schönberg the composer, and what they were supposed to mean and what they had to do with the naive pictures of Henri Rousseau, hung beside them, was as puzzling as Marc's leaping *Yellow Cow* and, particularly, Kandinsky's abstract *Composition*. Even well-meaning critics found it difficult to follow these stylistic leaps. Kandinsky and his friends were striving for a healing through art, but through a deeply felt spiritual art, which they discerned in many different forms of artistic expression. Kandinsky's "Concerning the Spiritual in Art" appeared just in time for the exhibition. In this work he tries to present what he sees as the new purpose of art. According to Kandinsky, the nightmare of materialism oppresses the soul of modern man – an idea that was in fact shared by many thinkers and artists of Kandinsky's time. Kandinsky wrote "Concerning the Spiritual in Art" in a mood influenced by idealist German philosophy (Kant, Fichte and Schelling), as well as by the usual anti-posi-

Der Blaue Reiter, 1911/1912
Title woodcut of the almanac
print from the black plate
Woodcut, 28 x 21.2 cm

Picture with a Black Arch, 1912
Bild mit schwarzem Bogen
Oil on canvas, 188 x 196 cm
Paris, Musée National d' Art Moderne,
Centre Georges Pompidou

DER
BLAUE REITER

Cover of the catalogue for the first
exhibition of the *Blaue Reiter,* after a
pen and ink drawing, 1911

tivist stance held in artists' circles. The essential insight into
man's new spiritual consciousness and the sense of a new age,
linked Kandinsky to Rudolf Steiner and the newly founded Anthro-
posophical Society. Religion and the occult were not just periphe-
ral interests for Kandinsky; in this period of searching and ques-
tioning they were his firm ground, and found their way into his
theory of art. There are verifiable indications of the direct expression of such mystical concepts in Kandinsky's pictures from before
the war. The theosophical classic by Annie Besant and C.W. Lead-
beater, which appeared in German translation as "Gedankenfor-
men" in 1908, supposedly led Kandinsky to the depiction of light
emanating in auras. He was concerned with making the spiritual
visible in abstract forms and colours. He tried to substantiate a secret, inner relationship between the stimulus of colour and its psy-
chological-spiritual effect on the viewer by applying the speculations which were current at that time, particularly among
Symbolist artists, about the relationships between various sensory
impressions. The mystical-cum-theosophical ideas about the "vibrations of souls" and "oscillation of fine substances" must in this
respect have seemed less a wrongheaded farrago to him than a
credible body of evidence.

According to Kandinsky all the arts, not just painting, were in
a state of spiritual renewal and were beginning to come closer to
their objective by turning to the abstract, the elemental. Above all
he cited the contemporary music of Schönberg as evidence of
this, but he also mentioned Wagner, Debussy, Scriabin, Schu-
mann and Mussorgsky. Among contemporary artists he singled
out the work of Matisse for its colours and Picasso for its forms.
The forerunners included the Pre-Raphaelite painter Dante Ga-
briel Rossetti; the German artist Arnold Böcklin; Giovanni Seganti-
ni, the neo-Impressionist; and Paul Cézanne, the seeker of new
principles of form and a pure means of painting. But this spiritual
renewal could only grow from a complete synthesis of all arts.
Until this epoch-making moment arrived, every art form would
have to devote itself to an examination of its individual elements.
As an example of this, Kandinsky dealt with the psychological effects of colour – one of the fundamental chapters in his theory of
art. He used his knowledge and experience of the synthesis of
sensory impressions to formulate a new harmonic theory of tones
of colour that maintain their tension by means of warm and cold
or light and dark contrasts. The new conception of colour and
form would ultimately result in pure painting: ". . . a mingling of
colour and form each with its separate existence, but each
blended into a common life which is called a picture by the force
of the inner need."

One of the earliest and best examples of refined composition
in this sense is *Composition V.* The sheer size suggests the vital
importance of this painting to Kandinsky. There are occasional,
rudimentary representational allusions between the totally abstract forms, for example in the city at the top edge of the picture,

and the rowing boat with three figures in primary colours. Kandinsky used similarly ambivalent images in the abstract paintings that followed during this period. These images, however stylized they may be, still point to a private iconography. All these elements allude to the theme of the Last Judgement, which, along with other similar themes like the Apocalypse, resurrection, destruction and rebirth, appeared again and again in Kandinsky's work before the war.

Kandinsky was aware of the dangers presented by a meaningless autonomy of form and colour: "If we begin at once to break the bonds which bind us to nature, and devote ourselves purely to combination of pure colour and abstract form, we shall produce works which are mere decoration, which are suited to neckties or carpets. Beauty of Form and Colour is no sufficient aim by itself . . ."

In his early abstract paintings Kandinsky tried to counteract this by using synaesthetic colour values and by finding forms

Untitled (First abstract watercolour),
1910 (1913)
Ohne Titel (Erstes Abstraktes Aquarell)
Pencil, watercolour and ink on paper,
49.6 x 64.8 cm
Paris, Musée National d'Art Moderne,
Centre Georges Pompidou

which would have an effect on the viewer precisely because they were still reminiscent of objective, representational images.

A beautiful example of this emotionally charged world of abstract forms is *Picture with a Black Arch* (p. 36). The dramatic composition of this piece is made up of three areas of shapes pressing against each other. From the bottom right-hand corner a shape, its colour intensifying into vermilion, rises towards the centre of the picture. A blue silhouette opposite presses forward, interspersed with heavily applied strokes and sprinkles of colour ranging from yellowish-white to reddish-orange. A violet-red disc shape rises over the red and blue. While the two lower sections are anchored to the edge of the picture, the form at the top moves freely over the surface flanked by smaller shapes of colour. The blend of red and blue producing violet seems to be trying to contain the tension-laden contrasts.

Of all the graphic elements running through the picture, the arch that gives it its title carries particular weight. The arch, which actually looks more like a right angle, frames all three shapes and reinforces the stabilizing function of the violet disc. But it can also be seen in terms of movement, starting in the red shape and, after bending slightly in the violet, moving down towards the blue. The black arch appears as an eruption of energy, as an image of violent struggle, in which the red forms represent one side and the retreating blue silhouette the other.

Kandinsky formulated one of the fundamental themes of his creative work in this central work of his Expressionist period – the theme of conflict and struggle, a theme which runs throughout his work, through his "Bauhaus" period and into the later pieces. In one of the more important chapters of "Concerning the Spiritual in Art" he gives what is practically a description (in anticipation) of this piece and the leitmotif that accompanies it. "Perhaps with envy and with a mournful sympathy we listen to the music of Mozart. It acts as a welcome pause in the turmoil of our inner life, as a consolation and as hope, but we hear it as the echo of something from another age long past and fundamentally strange to us. The strife of colours, the sense of balance we have lost, tottering principles, unexpected assaults, great questions, apparently useless striving, storm and tempest, broken chains, antitheses and contradictions, these make up our harmony."

The depiction of (artistic) conflict was not just one of many themes; it was the central theme posed by the time, Kandinsky lived in, torn as they were by contradictions. His aim was the representation of provocative contrasts of colour, not harmony. This is evident in the red and blue of *Picture with a Black Arch*. Colours were not just a creative device, they achieved an all-embracing power of expression drawing upon every sphere of knowledge and experience. "The unbounded warmth of red has not the irresponsible appeal of yellow, but rings inwardly with a determined and powerful intensity. It glows in itself, maturely, and does not distribute its vigour aimlessly."

"Blue is the typical heavenly colour. The ultimate feeling it creates is one of rest." In such observations Kandinsky ascribes to colour a psychological-cum-physical character capable of expressing experience. In place of figures and objects, colours now act as physiognomical characters on the stage of the painting. They are also animated by Kandinsky's vivid use of linear expression, which he examines in detail in a later publication entitled "Point and Line to Plane". Colour, line and freely flowing form combine to make up a dramatical visual idiom which expresses the antagonism between matter and spirit, and translates the entire eschatological mood of those years into an abstract but directly accessible iconology.

Improvisation 26 (Oars), 1912
Improvisation 26 (Rudern)
Oil on canvas, 97 x 107.5 cm
Munich, Städtische Galerie im
Lenbachhaus

This conflict was what "Der Blaue Reiter" was about. Kandinsky masked the naming of the group in a harmless, joking, coffee table anecdote. But blue was the "typical heavenly"–and therefore spiritual-colour for Kandinsky as well as for Marc. The theme of the rider, as we have already seen, also appears in many variations in Kandinsky's work and indicates a new aesthetic in its transformation from fairy tale prince to battling knight. The image of Saint George appears repeatedly in the almanac and transforms this motif in a Christian sense, as demonstrated in many of Kandinsky's verre églomisé pictures. The battle with the dragon stands for the triumph of the spiritual over the materialist view of the world, a hope which is expressed in the almanac in a variety of ways. Just as at the exhibition, the impartial observer leafing through the pages of the book would at first be confused by the wealth of diverse impressions. Bavarian votive and verre églomisé pictures were to be found alongside woodcuts from the Middle Ages, Chinese paintings, a mosaic from St. Mark's in Venice, sculpture from Mexico, Cameroon and the Easter Islands, Japanese pen-and-ink drawings, Russian folk prints and Egyptian shadow-play figures. The choice of contemporary painters was extended on the advice of Reinhard Piper, the enterprising Munich publisher, to include Vincent van Gogh, Henri Matisse and Paul Gauguin. And so, in addition to the work of the "Blaue Reiter" the almanac also contained reproductions of work by almost all the major modern artists. There were also contributions of modern music by Schönberg, Anton von Webern and Alban Berg, as well as Kandinsky's first piece for the theatre entitled "The Yellow Sound". Kandinsky also wrote the most important essays, "Concerning the Question of Form" and "Concerning Writing for the Stage". In "Spiritual Wealth," Marc lamented man's inertia in acquiring new spiritual insights. Macke's contribution, "The Masks", dealt with the secret of forms and the expression of inner life be-

Draft for *Picture with White Border,*
1913
Pencil, 15 x 25 cm
Munich, Städtische Galerie im
Lenbachhaus

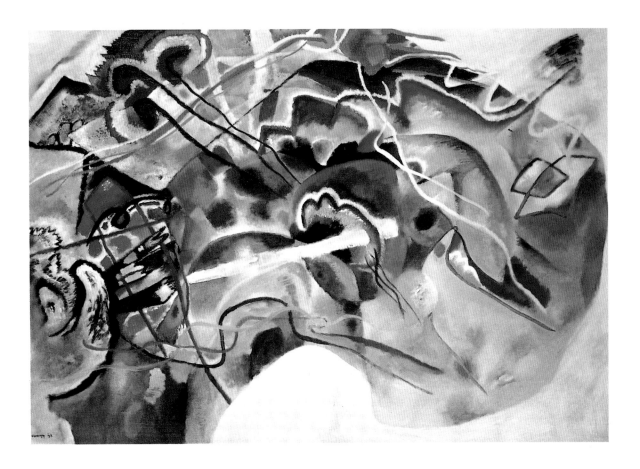

Picture with White Border, 1913
Bild mit weißem Rand
Oil on canvas, 140.3 x 200.3 cm
New York, The Solomon
R. Guggenheim Museum

hind them. David Burliuk reported on the "Savages of Russia", and Thomas von Hartmann, a composer and friend of Kandinsky's, wrote about "Anarchy in Music".

Arnold Schönberg wrote on the relationship between music and text, using the example of "Schubert's Lieder". Roger Allard's essay "Signs of Renewal in Painting" is devoted to the important new French Cubists, to whom Kandinsky had given a great deal of space in the Society shows. "Robert Delaunay's Methods of Composition" were dealt with in an analytical text by Erwin Busse. The French painter, who along with Kandinsky and other artists was seeking "pure art", had made a great impression on the "Blaue Reiter" circle with his idiosyncratic Eiffel Tower pictures and cityscapes.

It is clear from the range of illustrations and themes presented in the almanac that Kandinsky and Marc understood the Blaue Reiter to be not just a new movement in painting in Germany, but rather a call for spiritual renewal in all spheres of art and culture. This was meant to include the recollection of mankind's "spiritual wealth" from the past.

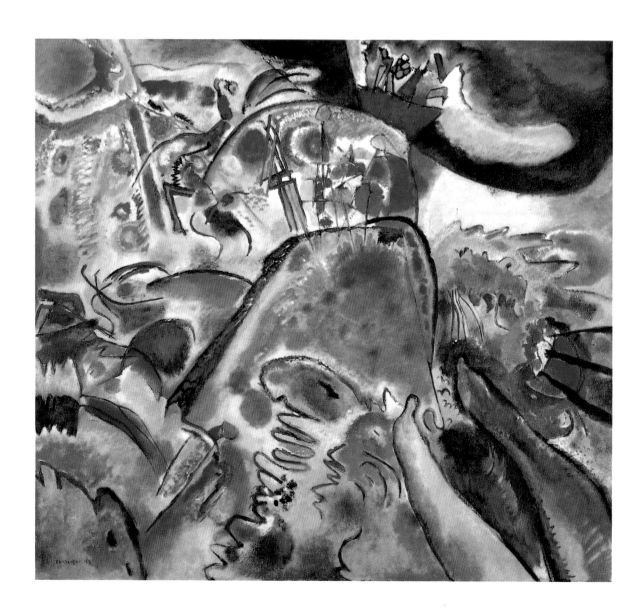

Small Pleasures, 1913
Kleine Freuden
Oil on canvas, 109.8 x 119.7 cm
New York, The Solomon
R. Guggenheim Museum

And so this almanac became a unique symbol of the changing direction in art that the forces of Modernism in all genres were bringing about throughout Europe. The success of these progressive stylistic trends benefitted the "Blaue Reiter" exhibitions. While the second exhibition, with over three hundred graphic works, followed at Hans Goltz's bookshop from 12 February to 18 March 1912, the first exhibition was taken on tour. It was first shown in the Gereonsclub in Cologne, then at Herwarth Walden's new Sturm gallery in Berlin. This was followed by the "Vereinigte Werkstätten für Kunst und Handwerk" ("Art and Craft Workshops") in Bremen, the Folkwang Museum in Hagen and the Salon Goldschmidt in Frankfurt am Main. Getting to know

Walden was especially important to Kandinsky, because Walden did his best to support new painting in his gallery and the publishing house associated with it. In October 1912 Kandinsky had his first individual exhibition at Walden's gallery. Kandinsky's essay, "Painting as Pure Art," appeared in *Der Sturm* magazine in 1913, and "Reminiscences", his biographical sketches, appeared in an album published by Walden entitled "Kandinsky 1901–1913". When the almanac finally appeared, published by Piper Verlag in May 1912, the "Blaue Reiter's" activity had already peaked. Although Marc expressed the wish for years thereafter to put together a follow-up edition, Kandinsky remained cool to the idea. In March 1914 he refused once and for all to take part in such a project. The "Blaue Reiter" editorial staff and artists' group existed for just a few years, but the two exhibitions and the almanac that appeared under this name were at the heart of twentieth century art. Many of the ideas that were first expressed there were developed further by the following generations of artists and some are still awaiting rediscovery.

For Kandinsky this active involvement in organizing exhibitions and making new contacts led to the decisive years on the road to abstract painting. The process which led from a gradual rejection of associative references to expression by means of pure colour and form can perhaps be best described by considering his "Improvisations". *Improvisation 26* follows on from the amorphous shapes and insinuating lines of his pictures of 1911. But one notices some ambivalent shapes in this picture as well, shapes which upon closer examination are recognizable as a representational use of form. And so the red patch on the right-hand side of the picture turns out to be a stylized figure which, in relation to the red arch and six black lines, suggests the rower in Kandinsky's accompanying explanation. The rowing boat, which appears in various transformations in many of his pictures dating from this period, is a part of Kandinsky's iconography and appears with particular clarity in *Small Pleasures* (p. 44) as a symbol of forward movement, like the rider motif, but also of the danger and sense of abandonment that man is exposed to. In some of these pictures he attempts the theme of Apocalypse and catastrophe as in, for example *Flood Improvization* (p. 47), one of the most colourful and turbulent of all Kandinsky's compositions. Every recognizable detail becomes lost in the eruptions of colour surging up and down; only in the upper left-hand corner of the picture does one seem to recognize the mountain, also one of Kandinsky's favourite basic motifs during this period. The mountain stands unshakeable in the midst of all this turmoil. Kandinsky was not alone in believing that the coming spiritual realm could only be reached by the most strenuous efforts. Many of his prophecies in "Concerning the Spiritual in Art" are based on "The Third Revelation", a twelfth century occult text by Joachim von Fiore. This text had been important to the Romantics and was discussed in the "Blaue Reiter" circle, particularly by Marc and Kandinsky.

Draft for *Small Pleasures*, 1913
Watercolour and ink on paper,
23.8 x 31.5 cm
Paris, Musée National d'Art Moderne,
Centre Georges Pompidou

Kandinsky and his circle expected a new age of the spirit to arise after the collapse of the materialist age. The appropriate form of expression for this new era was abstract painting, a means of expression Kandinsky was hard at work on.

Among these developments, two pictures stand out like a rest, a break, a memory of happy times. One is entitled *Gorge Improvisation* (p. 55) and shows, amid rising and falling cataracts of colour, a couple in Bavarian costume on a landing-stage with rowing boats to complete the picture. Whether Kandinsky was thinking about a trip with Gabriele Münter to one of the picturesque gorges near Garmisch-Partenkirchen, or whether he wanted to add an ironic footnote to the Futurist creed ("We put the observer in the middle of the picture" – First Futurist Manifesto, 1912) is not clear. Nevertheless, it demonstrates Kandinsky's lighter side amid the pictures of doom and catastrophe, a side emphatically acknowledged by those who knew him. The other painting that makes this relaxed impression is *Small Pleasures* (p. 44), a picture he also did as a watercolour (p. 45) and verre églomisé picture. Representational elements predominate in the tranquillity and reserved colours of the composition. A city on a mountain top is clearly recognizable, and perhaps a settlement (cf. *Colourful Life*) as well as suggestions of landscape, thundering riders, sha-

Dreamy Improvisation, 1913
Träumerische Improvisation
Oil on canvas, 130.7 x 130.7 cm
Munich, Staatsgalerie moderner Kunst

Flood Improvisation, 1913
Improvisation Sinflut
Oil on canvas, 95 x 150 cm
Munich, Städtische Galerie im
Lenbachhaus

dowy forms (giants?) at the foot of the mountain, and a cockle-shell boat with three rowers on a body of water on the right. The painting is most likely a reference to Kandinsky's love of "Mother Moscow", particularly in the light of his early pictures in which similar motifs appear. *Small Pleasures* seems like a form of recollection amid a hectic period of organizing exhibitions and continuing to develop new means of abstract expression in painting.

One of the milestones along the way was certainly *Picture with White Border* (p. 43), which he completed in 1913 at the height of his powers before the outbreak of World War I. He started making sketches for this painting after his return from Russia shortly before Christmas 1912. Again he recalled his leitmotif: St. George and the dragon. In numerous preparatory sketches and early draughts he worked the original motif into more and more abstract form until in the final version of the oil painting his "technique simply, straightforwardly and clearly" expresses what Kandinsky saw as the fundamental action of the picture, a "battle in white and black". The washed-out blue shape in the middle of the picture must be interpreted as a fighting figure, and the white line moving away from this shape as the lance which is directed at the "dragon", a striding black figure in the lower left-hand side of the painting. An important feature of the composition is the

Composition sketch for *Black Strokes*,
1913
Black chalk, grey background sheet,
21 x 20.5 cm
Munich, Städtische Galerie im
Lenbachhaus

Black Strokes I, 1913
Schwarze Striche I
Oil on canvas, 129.4 x 131.1 cm
New York, The Solomon R.
Guggenheim Museum

white border which surrounds the composition and concentrates
our attention on the essential parts of the painting.

One of Kandinsky's most successful paintings of this period
is *Dreamy Improvisation* (p. 46). Shapes of various colours surge
and soar around a blue centre on a diffuse ground colour. They
are accompanied by the "second voices", linear symbols and a
scattering of graphic elements which appear on equal terms as
completely independent contrapuntal shapes alongside the freely
applied colours. The entire composition radiates a serene, peaceful atmosphere far removed from the convulsive spasms of other
"Improvizations". In this picture Kandinsky walked the thin line
between the extremes of "dead" abstraction: "This way lies today
between two dangers. On the one hand is the totally arbitrary application of colour to geometrical form – pure patterning. On the
other hand is the more naturalistic use of colour in bodily form –
pure fantasy."

Perhaps this picture, with its oscillating colours and expressive symbols, shows most clearly what the expression "resounding cosmos" meant to Kandinsky – a lively network of relationships composed of free colour and form, freed in the final
analysis from representational associations, in the open space of
a painting. *Black Strokes* (p. 49) shows the same degree of play
between free floating colours and graphic symbols embedded in
them. The contrast between glowing streaks of colour and the
characteristic graphic style is even more clearly pronounced here
and is reminiscent of Japanese calligraphy, which Kandinsky admired all his life. Perhaps this richness of graphic invention was,
along with his sense of colour, Kandinsky's strength. This painting can almost be considered an early example of informal painting in the spirit of Wols' nervous style of drawing.

Incidentally, Kandinsky's so-called *First Abstract Watercolour
(Untitled)* (p. 39), dated 1910, is also similar in style to these paintings. In its free graphic style it resembles a preliminary sketch for
the great *Composition VII* 1913.

Kandinsky described the creation and meaning of *Composition VI* (p. 50) in greater detail than any of his other paintings. He
mentions the Flood as his starting point, a theme he had already
dealt with in more representational form in a glass painting. After
doing many preliminary sketches he finally attempted the actual
painting. In "Reminiscences" he writes: "One sees two centres in
this picture: first, on the left, a tender, pink, somewhat diffuse
centre with weak shaky lines in the middle, and second, on the
right (a little higher than the left), a coarse red-blue centre, somewhat discordant, with sharp, strong, very precise and rather male-
volent lines. Between these centres is a third (closer to the left),
which can only later be recognized as a centre but nevertheless
is ultimately the main centre. Here the pink and white froth in
such a way that they seem neither to lie on the surface of the canvas nor on any idealized surface. They seem to be floating in air,
surrounded by vapour . . .

Composition VI, 1913
Komposition VI
Oil on canvas, 195 x 300 cm
Leningrad, Hermitage

The person standing in the vapour is neither near nor far; he is just somewhere. This somewhere of the main centre determines the tone of the whole painting."

The composition of the painting is reminiscent of *Flood Improvisation* in the choice of colour and in some of the elements of the composition, such as the bundles of lines at the top and the right of the picture. After creating an impression of "inner nature", as Kandinsky defined "Improvisation", the internal action of the picture was refined via the glass painting into the big, sweeping "Composition", "a statement formed slowly and deliberately about the inner world of imagination and feeling." The pivotal (inner) motif of the Flood (apocalyptic atmosphere, preparation for the dawning of the spiritual age) is completely assimilated by the abstract means of expression and is "transformed into an inner, independent, objective entity of pure painting".

Composition VI was Kandinsky's most important work in the famous "Erster Deutscher Herbstsalon", which was organized by Herwarth Walden in Berlin in September 1913. It was modelled on the annual "Salon d'Automne" in Paris with its survey of the latest trends in art. For the radical "Blaue Reiter" painters it was again an opportunity to show their work in a large-scale exhibition of international prominence. The most impressive paintings in the exhibition were by Kandinsky, Marc and Macke, who together with Walden and Bernhard Köhler, a collector in Berlin, were responsible for the organization of the exhibition. The most important pictures were Kandinsky's *Composition VI, Picture with White Border* and *Picture with White Shapes*, Macke's *Four Girls, Zoological Garden* and *Girls Bathing*, and Marc's *Tower of Blue Horses* (lost), *Tyrol* and *Animal Destinies*. Along with the work of some Cubists and Futurists from Paris and Italy, including Jean Metzinger, Albert Gleizes, Fernand Léger, Umberto Boccioni, Giacomo Balla and Gino Severini, twenty-two works were dedicated to the memory of the late Henri Rousseau.

There was also a graphics cabinet with about twenty pieces each by Kubin and Paul Klee. The only work by an Expressionist artist was some drawings of nudes by Oskar Kokoschka. The "Brücke" artists did not take part, giving their participation in the Sonderbund exhibition in Cologne as the reason. The real reason, however, was more likely the growing animosity between the two groups; the "Blaue Reiter" tended more strongly towards abstraction and "Die Brücke" favoured an "art of Man". The actual focal point of the "Herbstsalon" was the paintings, designs and decorations of Sonia and Robert Delaunay, whose work had already been in the first exhibition and in the "Blaue Reiter" almanac through the agency of the painter Elisabeth Epstein. Robert Delaunay's dynamic "cityscapes" and "Eiffel Tower scenes" had already aroused great interest, but his new abstract series of "window pictures" and "circular forms" prompted unanimous enthusiasm among the "Blaue Reiter" painters. Delaunay had given form to "pure colour" without decorative trappings or graphic elements. After visiting the Delaunays with Marc in the autumn of 1912, Macke told of his fascination with the window pictures. "Reflecting mirror discs through which one sees the city and the Eiffel Tower on a sunny day, deep violet reflections, glorious orange on the right, pale blue houses at the bottom, from which the green tower, caught again and again in the sharply contrasting glistening of the disc, rises to the azure sky. That is the apparent, in fact very simple process. But to what tones he simplifies this simple motif. You must particularly see how the colours take on a wonderful depth as you step back. It is all so magnificently balanced that the whole of sunny Nature is reflected there . . ."

After meeting Delaunay again as a result of the "Herbstsalon", Macke began to turn more strongly to "pure colour" and therefore to reject Kandinsky's mystification. For Marc, too, the circular forms of 1913 signified a new means of articulating images, which, in his own way, he used right up to his very last works.

If Kandinsky was in any way stimulated by Delaunay's work, it was most likely in its confirmation of his own course towards the autonomy of pictorial elements. The absolute priority of "pure

Composition VII, 1913
Komposition VII
Oil on canvas, 200 x 300 cm
Moscow, State Tretjakov Gallery

colour", which Delaunay considered more important than all other pictorial functions, did not mean as much to Kandinsky. Nevertheless, one can see how strong his initial fascination with Delaunay's work must have been in some abstract colour studies that are ample proof of Delaunay's influence.

But Kandinsky took a different path in his "Compositions" – one in which many influences left their mark but were always transformed by the originality of Kandinsky's thinking about art.

The major work of Kandinsky's Munich period is without doubt *Composition VII* (p. 52), not only because of the great number of preliminary works, such as *Study for Composition VII (draft 2)* (p. 53), but also because of the complexity of themes and motifs. The preliminaries to this huge painting included about fifteen variants in the form of verre églomisé pictures, drawings, watercolours, woodcuts and oil paintings based on related themes. All of them revolve around eschatological themes such as the Flood, Resurrection and the Last Judgement. Kandinsky produced over thirty drawings and watercolours just for this painting, ranging from meticulous detail studies to sketches for the whole composition. He also produced at least ten oil paintings as studies. Several of these can be viewed as finished works in their own right.

According to Münter's diary the actual completion of the two by three metre painting took only three days. In spite of the intensive preliminary work the composition retains the freshness and spontaneity of the first sketches. A world of ideas explodes from the more graphically applied centre of the painting. Kandinsky was seldom in better form. Completely muted, hazy tones are suspended alongside jarring contrasts of colour. Simple shapes alternate with highly complex ones. There is no repetition of form or colour combination. From the currents and counter-currents Kandinsky creates a symphony of motifs and forms of expression, the final apotheosis of "Concerning the Spiritual in Art".

The publication of the long planned *Klänge*, a book of poems and woodcuts, by Piper Verlag closed this very fruitful period. 1914 began with the hope that *The Yellow Sound* would be performed at the Munich Artists' Theatre, but after intensive preparatory work with his friends from the "Blaue Reiter" circle, August Macke, Franz Marc and Alfred Kubin, the project had to be abandoned. The premiere of *The Yellow Sound* did not take place until 1982 at the Marymount Theatre in New York.

However, Kandinsky did at last have the opportunity to create an aesthetic environment, an idea that had been in his mind since his "Phalanx" days. He was commissioned by Edwin R. Campbell, an industrialist who had seen some of Kandinsky's work at the Armory Show in New York, to paint four murals for the foyer of his flat in New York. With the completion of these pictures in Murnau in the summer of 1914, Kandinsky finished the first, expressionist stage of his development towards abstraction. He moved with complete confidence through old motifs of form

Study for *Composition VII (Draft 2),* 1913
Studie zu Komposition VII (Entwurf II)
Oil on canvas, 100 x 140 cm
Munich, Städtische Galerie im Lenbachhaus

From Sounds, 1913
Woodcut, 16.3 x 21 cm

Gorge Improvisation, 1914
Improvisation Klamm
Oil on canvas, 110 x 110 cm
Munich, Städtische Galerie im
Lenbachhaus

and tones of colour, applying them in a free interplay of elements. The panels could not be shipped to New York until 1916, where two of them can today be found in the Guggenheim Museum.

Kandinsky was at the height of his creative powers, a respected artist and leading figure in the new genre of abstract painting, which he had established. In a series of small steps he had discovered a new concept in painting. He had carefully removed the representational elements from his compositions and transferred the subject matter conveyed by these elements to the "distinctive contours" of colour and form. In 1910 Kandinsky had already described the new subject matter of his paintings in the catalogue for the second Society exhibition: "The expression of mystery by means of mystery. Is that not the content? Is that not the conscious or unconscious purpose of the compulsive urge to create? . . . Man expresses the superhuman to Man – this is the language of art."

Kandinsky achieved the triumph of mystery and the spiritual in his paintings at least. He saw his works as a sweeping remedy for the sick times he lived in, not just as autonomous creations of the spirit. But the times were anything but peaceful. The outbreak of World War I, which was to affect the course of art history as radically as it changed society and thought in general, took Kandinsky and Münter by surprise in Murnau. On 3 August they fled to Goldach near Lake Constance, where Kandinsky continued working on his *Violet Curtain.* He then went alone to Moscow via Zurich. A last meeting with Münter in Moscow in the winter of 1915/16 ended not only an old friendship but rounded off one of the most exciting and eventful periods in the history of modern art.

Russian Intermezzo
1914–1921

Kandinsky was familiar with the artistic situation in Russia, having maintained many contacts in his old homeland. From 1902 on he had regularly sent essays and reviews of exhibitions from Munich to *World of Art*, a journal in St. Petersburg, and later to its successor *Apollo*. *World of Art* had an international editorial staff from all walks of intellectual life and they reported on the state of artistic affairs in Europe and Russia. A recurring theme in this journal was the relationship between music and painting kindled by Scriabin's "keyboard of light" and the discovery of Mikolai Ciurlionis, a Lithuanian painter, who had already tried to transpose music into semi-abstract painting at the turn of the century. When Ciurlionis moved to St. Petersburg in 1909, he received a tumultuous welcome as a "painter of synthesis" from the Symbolist artists there.

But more important to Kandinsky were his contacts to the members of the "Blaue Rose" ("Blue Rose"), a Symbolist artists' association in Moscow, whose exhibitions he took part in from 1900 to 1908 and again in 1911. The "Blaue Rose" artists agreed with Kandinsky on many points such as emphasizing colour as a "tonal medium" to construct rhythm and melody in a painting, and most of all in stressing the imaginative urge to create, divorced from representational portrayal. Vladimir Mayakovsky, the poet and critic, wrote in a review of the Blue Rose exhibition in 1907: "The artists are in love with the music of colour and line. They are heralds of primitivism, to which modern painting has come in search of rebirth at its source – in spontaneous creation, unburdened by the ballast of historical experience."

A fundamental shift of artistic standards took place in Russia between 1907 and 1908. The validity of the Symbolist view of art was increasingly called into question. A search began for immediate, intense sources of inspiration. "Karo Bube", a new artists' group, including the Burliuk brothers, as well as the painters Natalya Goncharova, Michail Larionov and Kasimir Malevich, found their first stimuli in Russian folk art but then quickly took their bearings from French art. The shared desire to find an elemental, primitive means of visual expression resulted in a short but fruitful collaboration between Kandinsky and the Moscow group. In 1910 Kandinsky invited the Burliuk brothers to take part in the second Society exhibition as well as the first and second "Blaue

"A work of art consists of two elements, the inner and the outer. The inner element on its own is the emotion of the artist's soul. This emotion is able to bring out a basically corresponding emotion in the soul of the viewer. As long as the soul is attached to the body, it can, as a rule, only receive vibrations transmitted by feelings. Feeling is also a bridge from the non-material to material (the artist) and from the material to the non-material (the viewer). Emotion – feeling – work – feeling – emotion."
Wassily Kandinsky

Moscow I, 1916
Moskau I
Oil on canvas, 51.5 x 49.5 cm
Moscow, State Tretjakov Gallery

Reiter" exhibitions, to which Goncharova and Larionov were also invited. In 1911 and 1912 he exhibited his own work in "Karo Bube" exhibitions in Moscow. Modern Russian art was also represented with texts and reproductions in the "Blaue Reiter" almanac.

The highpoint of Kandinsky's reception in pre-revolutionary Russia was certainly his presentation of the Russian version of "Concerning the Spiritual in Art" at the Second All-Russian Artists' Congress in St. Petersburg in December 1911. The Russian translation was finally published in 1914 and made Kandinsky's artistic principles available to a wider public. His arguments concerning the expressive power of pictorial elements formed the basis for his teaching activities in Russia and later in the Bauhaus. The Russian edition also included a geometrical diagram demonstrating the interrelations between various fundamental shapes and colours. The examination of these relations with regard to the psychology of perception and the theory of colour was the focus of Kandinsky's teachings at Russian art institutions and the Bauhaus.

But the Futurist manifesto "A slap in the face of public taste," published in December 1912, made it clear how remote Kandinsky's preoccupation with abstract motifs in the use of colour in painting was from the more radical efforts of the Russian avant-garde. After reading it Kandinsky complained to the editors, among them the Burliuks and Mayakovsky, about the inclusion of four of his poems from *Klänge*. These late symbolist poems, influenced by Maurice Maeterlinck, a writer Kandinsky greatly admired, were indeed out of step with the provocative tone of the manifesto, which rejected every romantic and sacred conception of art. Kandinsky's interest in theosophy, the occult and religion in its broadest sense, an interest expressed in "Concerning the Spiritual in Art", could only serve to alienate him from the Russian avant-gardists. Nikolai Punin's criticism of Kandinsky on the occasion of the Exhibition of Modern Russian Art in Petrograd was indicative of the growing rejection and isolation of Kandinsky among the new Formalists such as Ivan Kliun, El Lissitzky, Alexander Rodchenko and Kasimir Malevich. "I am not alone in believing in the deep, absolute seriousness of this painter. I also believe that this man has talent. Nevertheless, Kandinsky's artistic achievements are insignificant. As long as his work remains in the sphere of pure Spiritualism he conveys certain impressions, but as soon as he begins to speak about the 'language of things' he becomes not only a bad craftsman (draughtsman, painter) but simply a vulgar and thoroughly mediocre artist, too."

In Punin's objection to Kandinsky's art, an objection the Russian avant-garde widely shared, there was a grain of truth, as his paintings of this period demonstrate.

But for the time being Kandinsky's life brightened up, after he met Nina de Andreevsky, the daughter of a general. They married on 11 February 1917. He wrote an enthusiastic letter to Ga-

In Grey, 1919
Im Grau
Oil on canvas, 129 x 176 cm
Paris, Musée National d'Art Moderne,
Centre Georges Pompidou

briele Münter, whom he had last seen on the occasion of her exhibition at Gummeson's in Stockholm in 1916: "I felt that my old dream was closer to coming true. You know that I dreamt of painting a big picture expressing joy, the happiness of life and the universe. Suddenly I feel the harmony of colours and forms that come from this world of joy."

Perhaps he was referring to the big oil painting, *Moscow I* (p. 56), one of his most interesting works from this not exactly productive period. The structure is similar to *Small Pleasures* (p. 44), which has already been discussed. The difference is that here the landscape is superseded by multi-storey buildings, bridges, domes and churches. As in the early work *Colourful Life* (p. 8) Kandinsky seems to want to address himself to all areas of life in this painting, both religious and worldly aspects, death and the belief in an afterlife. The hopeful, optimistic aspects predominate in this period, which is evident in the naive, bright colours as well as in the couple in the middle of the picture, who appear to be uplifted in an aura, reminiscent incidentally of the couple in *Gorge Improvisation* (p. 55) from 1914. Stylistically Kandinsky

Red Oval, 1920
Rotes Oval
Oil on canvas, 71.5 x 71.5 cm
New York, The Solomon
R. Guggenheim Museum

was again coming closer to his early work. Semi-representational, fairy tale scenery dominates – along with warm bright colours applied in contrasting strokes. His other paintings of this period produce a similar effect, ranging from the optimistic to the naive. Perhaps after the subject matter of his "Blaue Reiter" catastrophe pictures, which in macabre fashion–but not at all in accordance with Kandinsky's intentions–had been so prophetic, he wanted to present a hopeful, joyful view of the future, a sort of paradise on Earth such as was promised by the new revolutionary forces. During the critical years of the Russian Revolution Kandinsky alternated between a tired, abstract idiom, post-Impressionist landscapes and naive-romantic fantasy pictures.

An increasing tendency toward making individual elements more geometrical becomes evident in the abstract works. On the one hand this development can be traced back to Kandinsky's own process of clarification, but on the other hand certainly to the avant-garde artistic climate in Moscow, dominated by Constructivists and Suprematists. In *Linear Colour Composition*, a watercolour dated 1920, the relation between the elements of colour and form seems playful and random rather than essential. A clearer answer to the work of his fellow Russian artists can be seen in *Red Oval* (p. 60). The centre dominating the picture consists of a yellow trapezoid, a complex shape creating a three-dimensional effect and a form used by the Suprematists in their work as well. But Kandinsky sets this surface against a richly modulated green background, thereby creating a curiously atmospheric space, in sharp contrast to the clarity and flatness of Suprematist paintings. He has also articulated a vocabulary of points, spots, lines and surfaces over the yellow shape, a vocabulary he was examining in his teaching activities. As an allusion to his Munich period there is also the hull of a boat and an oar projecting into the green surrounding area.

These and other works from his Soviet period lack the strength and determination of the Munich years. But in spite of the artistic doldrums and isolation Kandinsky found himself in, he was included in the development of cultural policy after the revolution. From 1918–1920 he was involved in art education and museum reform in an organization called IZO (Department of Fine Arts) which was part of NARKOMPROS (People's Commissariat for Cultural Education). He also published six long essays in 1919 and 1920, worked on an account of his own character, and started editing the first volume of an Encyclopaedia of Fine Arts which, however, was never published. As an expert for the state commission for acquisitions at the Museum of Pictorial Culture, which was supposed to open branches in many other Russian cities, he was also responsible for the selection and distribution of works of art. But his greatest sphere of influence was as head of a workshop at the Moscow SVOMAS (Free State Art Workshops). During his professorship, commencing in October 1918, he conceived a special curriculum based on the analysis of colour and form, a continuation of the ideas expressed in "Concerning the Spiritual in Art". In connection with these teaching activities he was also responsible for the organization and direction of the Moscow Institute for Artistic Culture (INChUK). The curriculum for INChUK was based in part on his earlier ideas about the interrelations of painting and music, and the analysis of fundamental forms and colours. But the leading figures on the staff, which was made up of the foremost Russian artists, parted company on this very point. His opponents Rodchenko, Stepanova and Popova stressed the precise analysis of materials in terms of constructive arrangement and conscious structuring. They rejected all irrationallity in the creative process. Kandinsky left INChUK shortly after is was founded to draft the curriculum for the physio-psychology department of RAChN (Russian Academy of Aesthetics) in 1921. However, he was not able to get very far, because he moved to Berlin at the end of 1921.

Between 1917 and 1921, in spite of growing resistance, Kandinsky was in a position to disseminate his art and his theory of art to a broad public. He took the curricula and the teaching methods he had tried out at INChUK to the Bauhaus, where they became a fundamental part of his teaching of art. Kandinsky took part in seven exhibitions during those years, gave many lectures and published essays about fundamental questions in the field of painting. Bolshevist pressure on the function and purpose of art started in 1922, and led finally to the establishment of Socialist Realism. Kandinsky's paintings were again removed from the museum and his work was no longer exhibited in the Soviet Union, a state of affairs which has only recently changed in a great Soviet retrospective. But the decisive factor leading to Kandinsky's departure was the constant hostility of his fellow artists, who saw only "spiritualistic deformities" (Punin) in his work. The increasingly geometrical nature of Kandinsky's paintings could hardly have been derived from contemporaneous Suprematist and Constructivist works. The dissimilarity is evident not only in the differing expressive uses of form but most of all in theoretical structure. The expressiveness with which Kandinsky analysed form distinguished him from the Russian Constructivists. A statement he made some time later makes the point: "The meeting of the pointed angle of a triangle and a circle is not less effective than the finger of God touching Adam's finger in Michelangelo".

In Kandinsky's work during this period the turbulent, glaring world of form and colour gives way to cool, rational composition based on the stricter analysis of form he was able to try out at the Russian art workshops. In a survey Kandinsky finally and emphatically disassociated himself from his Constructivist critics: "Just because an artist uses 'abstract' methods, it does not mean that he is an 'abstract' artist. It doesn't even mean that he is an artist. Just as there are enough dead triangles (be they white or green), there are just as many dead roosters, dead horses or dead guitars. One can just as easily be a 'realist academic' as an 'abstract academic'. A form without content is not a hand, just an empty glove full of air."

White Stroke, 1920
Weißer Strich
Oil on canvas, 98 x 80 cm
Cologne, Museum Ludwig

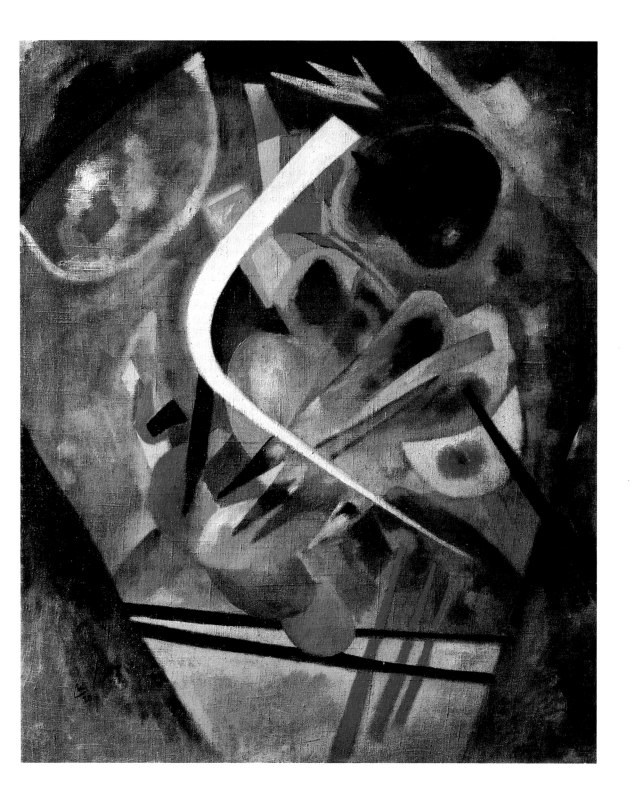

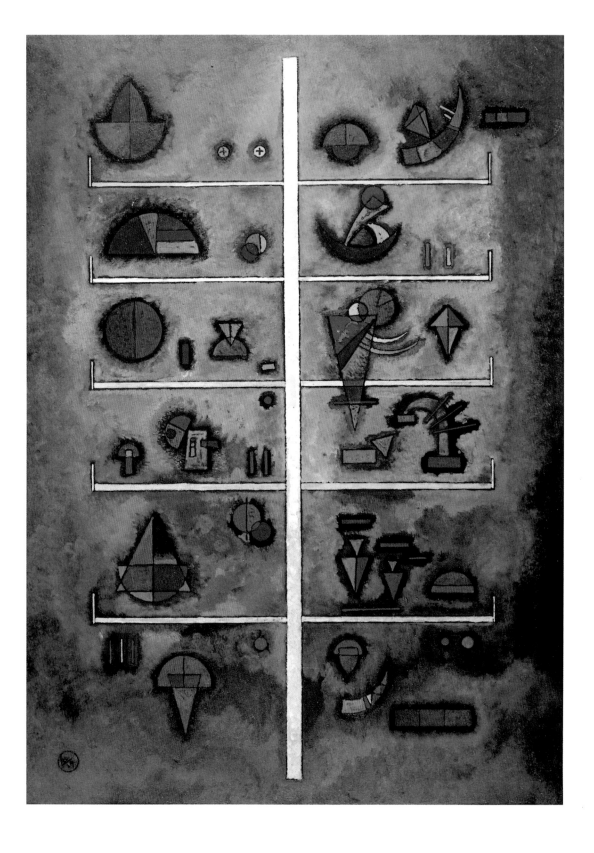

Point and Line to Plane: Kandinsky at the Bauhaus 1922–1933

Kandinsky's return to Germany, first of all to Berlin, took place in difficult circumstances. He could take only a few paintings with him, and nearly all the paintings he had left in the care of Walden had been sold at extremely low prices, the money having been devalued by inflation anyway. In the beginning he was as isolated in Berlin as he had been in Moscow. His friends were either dead, like Marc and Macke, who were killed in the war, or they lived elsewhere. Paul Klee and Lyonel Feininger were already teaching at the Bauhaus in Weimar. The art scene in Berlin was dominated by the "Neue Sachlichkeit" (New Objectivity), Expressionism and Dada, trends that were opposed to abstract painting. Kandinsky had already distanced himself from politically committed art in Moscow. He renewed the confrontation with his fellow artists from Russia with mixed feelings in the First Russian Art Exhibition, which took place at the van Diemen Gallery in Berlin at the beginning of 1922. Important as this exhibition was to the Constructivists and other Soviet artists, it did not change Kandinsky's position. He was a loner between all the radical styles that he rejected as either "formalist" or "ideological". And so the offer from Walter Gropius, the founder of the Bauhaus, to go to Weimar was all the more welcome.

Shortly before leaving Berlin, Kandinsky painted four murals for the Unjuried Berlin Art Show. These pictures were like a last reminiscence of his Moscow period but also a stocktaking of the new tasks that lay before him. *Mural B* (p. 66) is particularly reminiscent of the world of form Kandinsky had taken with him to Moscow from his brilliant Munich period, although he was no longer able to sustain the high emotional tension of that world. The technique of tempera on a black ground links the work to his Munich period. Painting these murals gave him a new opportunity to render in free form his concept of a synthesis of the arts.

This idea of a common basis for the arts, an idea he had carried with him since his "Blaue Reiter" days, was bound to bring him into spiritual proximity at least with the early, Expressionist phase of the Bauhaus.

The Bauhaus was a new type of art college. It was founded by Walter Gropius with the goal of bringing together the free and

Festival of Kites, 1922
Drachenfest
Woodcut, 15.6 x 10.5 cm

Storeys, 1929
Etagen
Oil on cardboard, 56 x 41 cm
New York, The Solomon
R. Guggenheim Museum

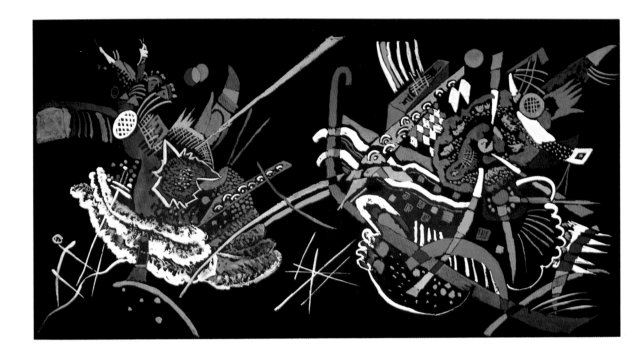

Draught for *Mural in the Unjuried Art Show, Wall B,* 1922
Entwurf für das Wandbild in der Juryfreien Kunstschau, Wand B
Gouache on black paper, mounted on cardboard, 34.7 x 60 cm
Paris, Musée National d'Art Moderne, Centre Georges Pompidou

applied arts in contemporary work founded on shared ideas of quality. The manifesto of 1919, the year of its foundation, states: "The ultimate goal of all visual artistic activity is construction! Architects, painters and sculptors must learn again to know and understand the multi-faceted form of building in its entirety as well as its parts. Only then will they of their own accord fill their works with the architectonic spirit they have lost in the art of the salon. Let us establish a new guild of craftsmen without the presumption of class distinctions building a wall of arrogance between craftsmen and artists. Together let us call for, devise and create the construction of the future, comprising everything in one form: architecture, sculpture and painting . . ."

Gropius called on some of the most modern and distinctive artists to teach the students at the Bauhaus in Weimar, among them Lyonel Feininger, Johannes Itten, Gerhard Marcks, Lothar Schreyer, Georg Muche, Oskar Schlemmer, Paul Klee and finally, in 1922, Kandinsky for the mural workshop. But more importantly for the moment, he was commissioned to teach a course about form for which Klee was also engaged. Here Kandinsky could again get involved in his old enthusiasm for teaching, and again take up his earlier ideas and develop them. This was particularly true of his more intensive analytical examination of individual pictorial elements, an analysis which he presented in print in "Point and Line to Plane" in 1926.

In his Bauhaus lessons Kandinsky leaned partially on the INChUK programme he had drawn up, but included new findings

from the emergent field of Gestalt psychology. In teaching colour
he stressed the polarity of yellow and blue, a principle he had
adopted from Goethe, and expanded on this with some characteri-
zations stemming from his theosophical and occult studies before
the war. The second contrast for Kandinsky was between black
and white, the third between green and red. Alongside the familiar symbolic classification of colours and their subdivision into
"four main tones", warm–cold and light-dark, Kandinsky concen-
trated more on the physical basis of the classification of colours
in his "Bauhaus" teachings and, above all, explored the colour
triad of yellow-blue-red. In connection with his work in the workshop for mural painting he dealt more intensively with paints and
various binders. In the charts of basic colour patterns, which
were often used in lessons, he was able to refer back to the
groundwork of Itten's teachings about colour in the preliminary
course (see colour wheel by Eugen Batz, p. 70).

Small Worlds III, 1922
Kleine Welten III
Colour lithograph, 27.8 x 23 cm
Munich, Städtische Galerie im
Lenbachhaus

Small Worlds VI, 1922
Kleine Welten VI
Woodcut, 27.1 x 23.3 cm
Munich, Städtische Galerie im
Lenbachhaus

Small Worlds VII, 1922
Kleine Welten VII
Colour woodcut, 27.1 x 23.3 cm
Munich, Städtische Galerie im
Lenbachhaus

But his teachings about form were essentially new, starting with an analysis of individual elements such as point, line and plane and then examining their relations to each other. His examination of the effects of forces on straight lines, leading to the contrasting tones of curved and angled lines, coincided with the research of Gestalt psychologists, whose work was also discussed at the Bauhaus. In a last section Kandinsky dealt with the classification of colours and forms as well as their relation to linear elements. He tried to substantiate his findings by means of systematic, analytical tasks. Nevertheless, the arrangement of basic forms and colours as taught by Kandinsky was more a product of subjective evaluation than of objectively verifiable laws. His concept of "correspondence" between colours and forms is based on similar ideas expressed in "Concerning the Spiritual in Art". Its source is the thoroughly unconstructive, mystical theories of the Symbolists. The only consistent application of this system of classification was in Herbert Bayer's design for the staircase of the Bauhaus.

Another course dealt with "Analytical Drawing": "Constructive" still lifes composed by students would be rendered in abstract linear drawings. Even if Kandinsky's lessons were not as exciting or as rousing as Itten's, who set up a sensational preliminary course but had to leave the Bauhaus in 1923 because of his mystical spiritualism, or his successor's, Josef Albers, Kandinsky nevertheless, with great clarity and consistency, made his students aware of the fundamental principles of visual art, princi-

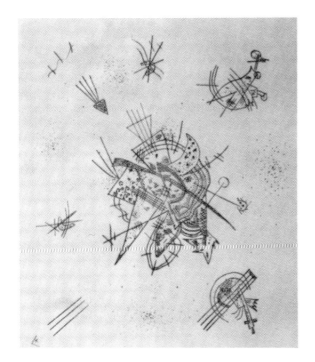

Small Worlds X, 1922
Kleine Welten X
Etching, 23.9 x 20 cm
Munich, Städtische Galerie im
Lenbachhaus

Small Worlds XI, 1922
Kleine Welten XI
Etching, 23.9 x 20 cm
Munich, Städtische Galerie im
Lenbachhaus

ples without which the artist cannot create. His paintings were accordingly marked by this logic and austerity. His "cool period" had begun in Moscow with *Red Spot II* (cf. pp. 92–3), but his purely constructive paintings were produced under the pressure of analytical teaching and the strong rational line of the Bauhaus programme which, after Itten's dismissal, steered a technical, functional course. In addition to this, the entire Bauhaus found itself drawn along in the undertow of a universal geometrical language between 1923 and 1925, a trend brought about by the increasing influence of the Suprematists and the Constructivists. For example, Itten's successor, László Moholy-Nagy, transformed the preliminary course into a course in constructive visual form.

Individual geometrical elements increasingly entered the foreground of Kandinsky's work. The passionate colours of the Munich and Moscow paintings gave way to a cool, occasionally disharmonious use of colour. The circle as a symbol of perfect form, but also as a cosmic symbol, was the focal point of his paintings of this period.

The main work of Kandinsky's Weimar period is a large painting entitled *Composition VIII* (p. 72). The geometrical vocabulary is limited to a few elements such as circle, semi-circle, angles, and straight and curved lines. The dominant circle is at the top left of the painting with other focal centres of coloured circles swirling about it. Chessboard-like latticed patterns cross through the free flight of the circles and semi-circles without restricting them or coming into confrontation with them. In this ambivalent,

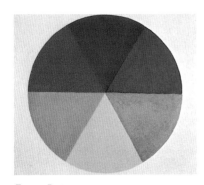

Eugen Batz,
Six-part Colour Circle, 1930
Sechsteiliger Farbkreis
estate of Eugen Batz

Several Circles, 1926
Einige Kreise
Oil on canvas, 140 x 140 cm
New York, The Solomon
R. Guggenheim Museum

suspended balance between the various parts of the picture lies the greatest difference to Kandinsky's earlier pictures. The earlier work is characterized by an elemental drama between colour and form, whereas the newer work seems to be worked out intellectually and therefore lacks tension. In the worst cases these pictures are like the decorative exercises Kandinsky had earlier warned about. In contrast, the twelve graphic prints of *Small World* (pp. 68–9), which Kandinsky produced for Propyläen Publishers just after his arrival in Weimar, are astonishingly imaginative. In a few weeks he produced four lithographs in colour; four woodcuts, two of them in colour; and four etchings containing a variety of techniques and compositions. While the colours are reduced primarily to yellow, red and blue, he experiments with various combinations of new elements of form – grid, chessboard, circle and wedge-forms, as well as shading in the etchings. *Small Worlds III* (p. 67) is an echo of the Munich paintings. Kandinsky tried out a sort of "basso continuo of painting", a grammar of pictorial elements he conceived at the Bauhaus for a new approach to painting. Alongside these official works he produced some private, more intimate pictures, such as *Small Dream in Red* (p. 74), which was a present for his wife. These paintings are more inspired and are imbued with life. *Small Dream in Red* consists of warm brownish tones and elements with slightly representational associations. The essential features and individual elements of the composition are borrowed from the 1912 *Improvisation 24.*

In addition to teaching courses, Kandinsky became actively involved in giving lectures and mounting exhibitions, which took him as far as the USA along with Feininger, Klee and Jawlensky.

This first phase of the Bauhaus ended in 1925, partly because of attacks by right-wing parties in Weimar. The second phase, in Dessau, began under fundamentally more favourable conditions. Funds were even made available for their own classroom building and masters' houses. The Klee and Kandinsky families lived next door to each other in a semi-detached house. Both painters had asked Gropius to set up free painting classes so they could again pursue their own work more intensively. Kandinsky's two most important paintings from these troubled years are *In Blue* (p. 73) and *Yellow-Red-Blue* (p. 75). *Yellow-Red-Blue* approaches the great Compositions in size and significance. The left half of the painting is light and bright, graphic and linear. The right is darker and heavier with more artistic ideas, like the dark blue circle and the curved black line. The "earthly" yellow stands for firmness, the "heavenly" blue seems to be floating away towards the top right. This contrast is, in its arrangement of colour and form, reminiscent of Kandinsky's earlier leitmotif of the knight and the dragon, both of which seem to reappear here in completely formalised configurations.

This painting may also represent Kandinsky's new attitude of "cool romanticism", which was to run through the constructive compositions of his Bauhaus paintings: "The circle, which I have

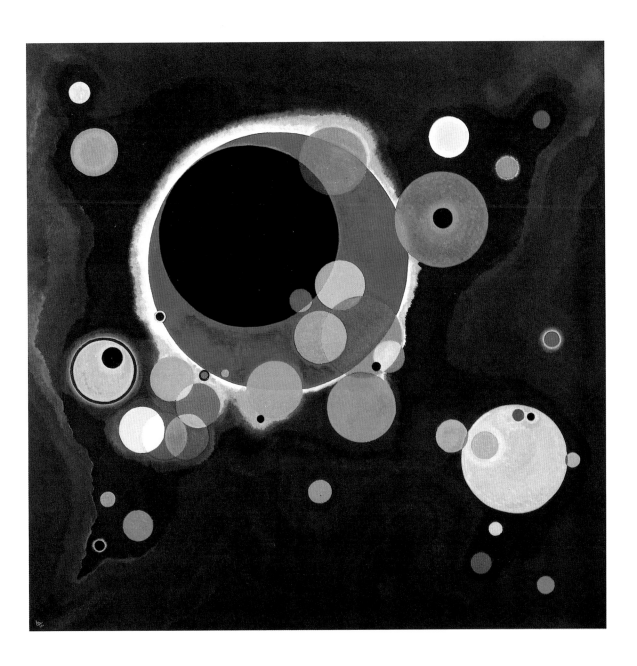

Composition VIII, 1923
Komposition VIII
Oil on canvas, 140 x 201 cm
New York, The Solomon
R. Guggenheim Museum

been using so often recently, can sometimes only be described as romantic. And the coming romanticism is indeed deep, beautiful, meaningful and joyful – it is a piece of ice with a flame burning in it. If people only sense the ice and not the flame, then it's all the worse for them . . ."

The most beautiful product of these thoughts is *Several Circles* (p. 71). A dark blue central circle, partially overlaid like an eclipse by another black circle, is surrounded by smaller and larger circles in radiant colours floating on a dark brown ground. New, finely differentiated tones of colour result from the overlapping of some transparent circles. At the Bauhaus, Kandinsky became acquainted with the use of transparency as a new technique of artistic expression in painting from the glass painting workshop, and especially from the experiments with light conducted by Ludwig Hirschfeld-Mack. Klee profited from this in his paintings as well.

The outward changes at the "Bauhaus" occurred alongside financial consolidation. The newly founded "Bauhaus GmbH" (Bauhaus Limited) saw to the social utilization of the products of the furniture workshop, as well as the lamps and the typography designed at the Bauhaus. Their greatest success came later – with

Bauhaus wallpaper! New synthetic fibres were tried out in Gunna Stölzl's textile department. The Bauhaus began increasingly to adapt itself to industrial production. The mural workshop was taken over in Dessau by Hinnerk Scheper who, in contrast to Kandinsky's monumental murals, focused on the problems of colour in the design of space and structure. Although Kandinsky had been the head of this workshop from 1922 to 1925, he had not been able to accomplish what he had set out to do. The most convincing manifestation of Kandinsky's concept of space, in which colour and form were supposed to correspond, was in the furnishings of his flat in Dessau. The multi-coloured living-room in light pink, ivory, black and grey – one corner was even coated with gold leaf – was like a painting the observer could enter, an idea Kandinsky had cherished since his first encounter with Russian folk art. The Bauhaus theatre, with Schlemmer's abstract figurines and elementary plots, came closest to Kandinsky's idea of an "abstract synthesis of the stage". But he wasn't able to put on "The Yellow Sound", his main theatrical work, here either.

In the final analysis his concept of synthesis remained too closely attached to the romantic idea of a "Gesamtkunstwerk," or total work of art, to fit in with the increasingly functional orientation of the Bauhaus towards design and architecture. All the same, in 1928 he was able to realize his conception of "artistic synthesis" in his visual accompaniment to Mussorgsky's "Pictures at an Exhibition". He wanted to accompany the movement of the musical phrases with moving shapes and lighting. Musical and visual expression were to mutually illuminate and intensify each

In Blue, 1925
Im Blau
Oil on canvas, 80 x 110 cm
Düsseldorf, Kunstsammlung
Nordrhein-Westfalen

other with discord and harmony. His ceramic wall sculpture for the construction exhibition of 1931 in Berlin must also be seen in this context. The motifs of the murals again combined the geometrical forms, abstract figures and symbols that Kandinsky explored and experimented with during his Bauhaus period.

There was a particularly strong tendency at the Dessau Bauhaus to "musicalize" visual material. Lectures and colloquiums were held on the subject, experiments with light and sound were carried out on stage, and Klee painted his "Fugue pictures" and "Polyphonies" – abstract settings of musical impressions. In "Concerning the Spiritual in Art" Kandinsky had already postulated an inner relationship between music and painting. In his "Bauhaus" paintings he now used visual elements from a musical standpoint – repetition, inversion, variation, dynamic intensification and diminution. *On the Points* is in effect an illustration of this principle. The composition leaves one with an emotional impression which is difficult to define, as if Kandinsky wanted to translate "the fanfares of Wagner", the hero of his youth and catalyst of intense experiences of artistic synaesthesia, into visual terms.

In the last years of the Bauhaus, Kandinsky again stressed more strongly the role of intuition in the creative process, without which no work of art could be produced. In 1928, in the journal "bauhaus 2/3", he described the important relationship between intellect and intuition: "The great epochs of art always had their teachings or theories, which were as self-evident in their

Small Dream in Red, 1925
Kleiner Traum in Rot
Oil on cardboard, 35.5 x 41.2 cm
Berne, Kunstmuseum Bern
gift of Nina Kandinsky

necessity as has been the case in science. These teachings could never replace the element of intuition, because knowledge in and of itself is barren. It must content itself with the task of providing material and method. Intuition is fertile in that it uses material and method as a means to an end. But the end cannot be achieved without the means and in this sense intuition is also barren".

Thus Kandinsky's works from the last years of the Dessau Bauhaus are light again, and have a rather droll sense of humour, pointing to his late work in Paris. Among these works is *Capricious* (p. 77), with its enigmatic associations between barque and spaceship, Egyptian hieroglyphics and Klee's dream-like symbolic language. There was a friendly sense of fellowship between Kandinsky and Klee, and they showed consideration for each other's artistic principles. They valued each other as people and painters but created different worlds. Klee's enthusiasm for experimentation with new materials and techniques seems to have found expression in Kandinsky's paintings mostly in the visual presentation and the spray technique of some of his pieces from this period. Klee considered Kandinsky his "friend and mentor" but based his writings and pictures on completely different principles of artistic creation, principles which he always saw as analogous with natural processes.

Yellow-Red-Blue, 1925
Gelb-Rot-Blau
Oil on canvas, 127 x 200 cm
Paris, Musée National d'Art Moderne,
Centre Georges Pompidou

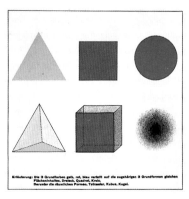

The three primary colours are arranged in the corresponding three basic forms (triangle, square, circle) of equal surface area, 1923
Berlin, Bauhaus Archives

Storeys (p. 64), a wondrous collection of abstract entities occupying the different floors of a house structure, is reminiscent of Klee's work. Perhaps these "storeys" are an ironic commentary on the construction programme of the Bauhaus, the functional structuring of living space into small, identical units like the experimental Törten estate in Dessau, built with the help of industrial production methods. Though Kandinsky's paintings may seem cheerful, the last years of the Dessau Bauhaus weren't: after Gropius resigned in order to concentrate on his architectural programme again, there followed a period of sharp politicization of the students under the direction of Hannes Meyer between 1928 and 1930. The conflict which had long been growing between the Bauhaus aesthetic, represented mainly by the painters, and a one-sided functional orientation now became open war. Meyer was socially committed and opposed to any form of aestheticism, and wanted to dispense with every "Bauhaus style, every Bauhaus fashion." To him the Bauhaus was above all "a higher school of form and structure" with clear social responsibilities.

The student body also split into two camps. Kandinsky and Klee found themselves exposed to fierce attacks because of their "ivory tower painting". In the end Meyer was dismissed from his post, and in the summer of 1930 architect Mies van der Rohe was appointed as director of the Bauhaus.

Mies van der Rohe was primarily interested in de-ideologizing the Bauhaus, above all because of intensifying attacks from radical right-wing circles. As a result, the Bauhaus developed into a purely architectural school, which no longer had anything to do with the aims of Gropius or of Kandinsky and Klee.

Klee readily took up an offer from the Düsseldorf Academy. Kandinsky withdrew more and more from teaching activities. In 1931 the Nazis started an intense campaign of malicious agitation against the Bauhaus, which ended with its closure in 1932. In October 1932 Mies van der Rohe re-opened the institution on his own responsibility in a disused telephone factory. But as early as April 1933 (shortly after Hitler came to power) the school was searched and temporarily closed by the Gestapo. On 19 July the staff resolved to close the Bauhaus for good. Many of the teachers and students emigrated to the USA and there disseminated the teachings of the Bauhaus. One was Gropius, who in 1937 started work at Harvard University where Marcel Breuer, a former student at the Bauhaus in Weimar and later head of a workshop, also taught. Josef Albers continued by developing the preliminary course at Black Mountain College, North Carolina. László Moholy-Nagy founded the New Bauhaus in Chicago.

Kandinsky and his wife were able to get away in time to Paris, where they moved into a newly-built flat in the suburb of Neuilly-sur-Seine. Kandinsky's years at the Bauhaus had been characterized above all by penetrating rational analysis of art work. His many writings, particularly "Point and Line to Plane",

are ample evidence of this. His paintings are marked by a strict, often rigid and disharmonic structure, which did not soften again until the end of the 1920s. Kandinsky's theories were still founded on a non-rational basis, seeing purely artistic laws, the tensions between colour and form, the emotional and spiritual qualities of visual elements, as requirements of an "inner necessity". Even during the Bauhaus period he did not forget the experiences and influences which had left their mark on him, his capacity for vividly concrete expression and for merging several different sensory impressions, or the occult speculations of "Concerning the Spiritual in Art". Instead he overlaid them with the rational vein of his teaching requirements and the changing pre-requisites of the Bauhaus idea. His work already heralded the later pieces produced in Paris, where a non-rational sense of play, a humorous vein and a symbolic language close to Surrealism broke through the façade of formal laws of structure, behind which Kandinsky's temperament, his romantic mystical vein, was still pulsing.

Capricious, 1930
Launisches
Oil on cardboard, 40.5 x 56 cm
Rotterdam, Museum Boymans-van
Beuningen

Biomorphic Abstraction:
Kandinsky in Paris
1934–1944

Kandinsky hoped to quickly resume contact with old friends and fellow artists, particularly since he had acquired an international reputation. The Paris art scene reacted to Kandinsky's arrival with extreme coolness and reserve, on the one hand by limiting the "School of Paris" to French artists and on the other by according abstract painting no recognition. The preferred stylistic trends lay between Impressionism and Cubism. The cool, geometrical means of expression represented in Paris by a few artists such as Piet Mondrian, Jean Arp and Georges Vantongerloo met with no success. After his contacts with the Russian emigrant scene in Paris came to nothing, Kandinsky limited his contacts to the handful of artists from his happy times.

One of these old friendships was with the Delaunays, whom he enjoyed visiting. Robert Delaunay's new series, "Rythmes sans fin" (Rhythms without end), appealed to Kandinsky's sense of colour and his special fondness for the circle. Among the new artists he admired only Joan Miró, Jean Arp and Alberto Magnelli, and he regularly went to their openings. But he was repelled by the constructive artists of the "Cercle et Carré", and particularly by Mondrian, because of their puritanism.

Otherwise he lived and worked in seclusion in a small flat, the living-room of which he had fitted out as a studio. In these modest surroundings he wrought the final transformation in his methods of visual expression. There can be no question of this being the quiet word of old age reviewing past glories. The most conspicuous transformation in these late paintings was in the use of colour. A singing, resounding play of colours in most subtly differentiated nuances rises from a cloud of colour, as can be seen in *Gentle Ascent* (p. 81). He seems to have left constructive theories about colour based on primary and secondary colours behind at the Bauhaus. He now uses combinations of colour never before seen in the world of art, most of them having a delicate filigree effect but also reminiscent of Slavic folk art in their colourfulness. The colours are applied thinly, sometimes transparently, so that they produce an added optical blending with other colours or the ground colour. A new technique is the use of sand, either mixed with paint or as a granular ground to catch the paint. The use of colour is most reminiscent of Kandinsky's early fairy tale pictures, which referred back to his memories of Moscow with its

Detail study from *Sky Blue*

Sky Blue, 1940
Himmelblau
Oil on canvas, 100 x 73 cm
Paris, Musée National d'Art Moderne,
Centre Georges Pompidou

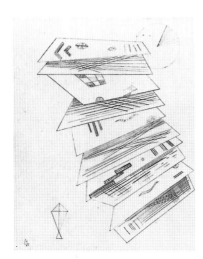

Second etching for *Editions Cahiers d'Art*, 1932
Etching, 29.8 x 23.8 cm
Munich, Städtische Galerie im Lenbachhaus

Gentle Ascent, 1934
Zarter Aufstieg
Oil on canvas, 80.4 x 80.7 cm
New York, The Solomon
R. Guggenheim Museum

multi-coloured and golden towers and roofs. Tones of colour based on primary colours or well-known contrasts are seldom used here. Bright, diverse, broken fields of colours which hardly follow conventional rules dominate. As if this new use of colour were not complicated enough, Kandinsky invented a new formal idiom to go with it. The basic geometrical forms dissolve into an unbelievable variety of shapes among which biomorphic ones predominate over those derived from geometrical shapes.

The large shapes of colour dominating the picture in *Violet Dominant* are clearly reminiscent of medusas, the deep-sea jellyfish. Other shapes create the impression of plankton and small microscopic aquatic organisms, as in *Composition IX* (p. 82) and especially *Sky Blue* (p. 78), in which a number of colourful forms and shapes are seen floating against a sky-blue background, like the view through a microscope into an unknown world. In an article in the Danish journal "Konkretion" (1935) Kandinsky expands on the concept of "vibrations of the soul" perceived by "inner sight": "This experience of the 'hidden soul' of all things that we see with the unaided eye, through a microscope or through a telescope, I call 'inner sight.' This sight penetrates the hard shell, the 'external' form, into the interior of things and lets us perceive the inner 'pulsation' of things with all our senses."

Kandinsky had already drawn attention to the analogies between art, nature and technology in his Bauhaus lessons. But he did not open his own use of expressive form to these insights until after arriving in Paris. These newly acquired resources of form were inspired by the most varied sources, from invertebrate sea creatures, the smallest of organisms and zoological prototypes to the embryological forms that populate many of his works in his late period between 1934 and 1940. His sources of inspiration included the paintings of his fellow artists in Paris as well as encyclopaedias and biological works such as Ernst Haeckel's "Kunstformen der Natur" (Art Forms in Nature) and Karl Blossfeldt's famous photo collection "Urformen der Natur" (Prototypes in Nature). Although Kandinsky was irritated by the comparisons with Jean Arp, Joan Miró and Alberto Magnelli, which the art historian Alfred Barr made in the foreword to the catalogue of the exhibition "Cubism and Abstract Art" (1936, Museum of Modern Art, New York), a certain interdependence must nevertheless be accepted. Jean Arp had already introduced biomorphic forms in sculpture in the 1930s. Miró had also been dealing with symbolic expression made up of abstracted forms. Shorthand symbols, like exclamation marks and commas, were borrowed from Klee's work, who at that time was working with precisely such an economical symbolic vocabulary. Incidentally, Klee was the only artist from the Bauhaus period who remained Kandinsky's friend until the latter's death in 1940.

Kandinsky's paintings of this period are not refined by "cool romanticism" or the wisdom of old age. Rather they are hot-

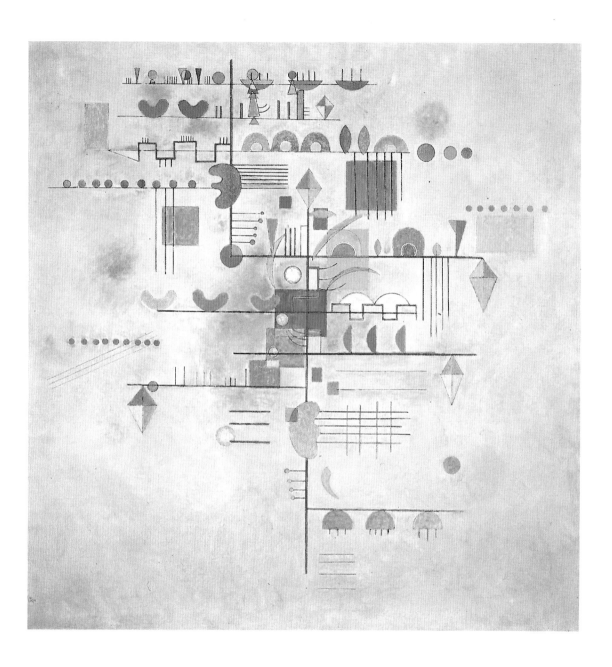

Composition IX, 1936
Komposition IX
Oil on canvas, 113.5 x 195 cm
Paris, Musée National d'Art Moderne,
Centre Georges Pompidou

headed, seething, primaeval, as if some distant sun were trying to set life flowing again with protoplasm in a pond. In this connection *Colourful Ensemble* (p. 87), with its variety of colourful protuberances, is a seminal painting. The geometrical forms and compositional structure, which Kandinsky had previously observed so strictly, have a hard time holding their own against this flood of mythical creatures. Only occasionally does he fall back on a firm, tectonic, visual pattern as in *Two Green Points* (p. 83) or in some of his half-tone pictures. From time to time the "creatures of colour and form" create a cheerful effect and lead a predominantly independent life on the cloudy, multi-coloured ground, as in *Complex-Simple* (p. 85) or *Sky Blue* (p. 78). He even uses a black ground again, as in *Composition X* (p. 88), Kandinsky's last big compostion before the outbreak of World War II. It creates a mythical, visionary visual world which, in its wealth of colour and form, shows no trace of the impending military conflict.

An example of the unwavering complexity of Kandinsky's work can be found in the big painting *Dominant Curve* (p. 84), a fireworks show of fantasy and complexity. A swarm of symbols and biomorphic shapes sweep over the once so coolly constructed circles. Some of these develop into a sort of picture scroll, a picture within a picture. The staircase-like construction on the right clearly refers to Kandinsky's knowledge about the psychology of perception. This tilting figure appears in some of Klee's works as well, in addition to some other pieces by Kandinsky (see for example the second etching for the *Edition Cahiers d'Art*, p. 80).

In the war years which followed, the format of Kandinsky's work became smaller until he had to be satisfied with working with gouache on small pieces of cardboard because of the acute lack of materials. In their structure and content, however, these works are on a par with his large compositions. The public and the critics were again taken aback by this explosion of form and colour, and this only served to increase Kandinsky's isolation in the Parisian art world. This artist, who had once been so lively and so openly involved in the politics of art, now depended on his few contacts, on the journals "Cahiers d'Art" and "XXe. Siècle," as well as on a few abstract artists such as the Abstraction-Création circle. This group, which followed "Cercle et Carré", a group of artists producing geometrical works, wanted to stand firm against the dominance of the Surrealists. But Kandinsky took up contact with the newly established Surrealist group. He had already met André Breton, who bought two watercolours from him, in the early 30s. So it is hardly amazing that in 1933 Kandinsky's work was also represented in the "Sixième Salon des Surindépendants" as a "leader of the Surrealist procession", as Jean Arp called him. For a time Kandinsky was even identified with the Surrealists, among whom more abstract artists such as Arp, Miró and André Masson were also to be found. Nevertheless, Kandinsky never lost sight of the fundamental difference between his work and that of the Surrealists. While the Surrealists affirmed the dictates of the unconscious and of psychoanalytical explanatory models, Kandinsky's "inner necessity" led him back to the principles of the psychology of perception and to his "inner voice", the "clockwork"

Two Green Points, 1935
Zwei grüne Punkte
Combined technique on canvas,
114 x 162 cm
Paris, Musée National d'Art Moderne,
Centre Georges Pompidou

Dominant Curve, 1936
Dominierende Kurve
Oil on canvas, 129.3 x 194.3 cm
New York, The Solomon R. Guggenheim
Museum

Complex-Simple, 1939
Kompliziert-Einfach
Oil on canvas, 100 x 81 cm
Paris, Musée National d'Art Moderne,
Centre Georges Pompidou

that had been the driving force of his artistic creativity since the early years. Breton's preference for representational depiction became more entrenched and this finally led to the break-up of the original Surrealist group. In order to divorce himself more strongly from "abstract" Surrealism, as well as from artists tending towards a strict geometrical style, Kandinsky increasingly fell back on the idea of "concrete art" in his writings. The expression had already been used by Theo van Doesburg in 1930, but was newly defined by Kandinsky for his own purposes.

"Abstract art places a new world, which on the surface has nothing to do with 'reality', next to the 'real' world. Deeper down it is subject to the common laws of the 'cosmic world,' And so a 'new world of art' is juxtaposed to the 'world of nature.' This 'world of art' is just as real, just as concrete. For this reason I prefer to call so-called 'abstract' art 'concrete' art."

Kandinsky was able to assert himself as a leading figure on the new international art scene just one more time. As a result of the growing dissatisfaction abstract and Surrealist artists felt in view of the one-sided composition of the annual survey of contemporary art at the Petit Palais, Kandinsky composed a strong polemic which led his friend André Dézarrois, curator of the Jeu de Paume, to mount an alternative exhibition, 'Origines et développement de l'art international indépendant' from 30 July to 31 October 1937. But mainly Cubist and Surrealist works were shown at Jeu de Paume, and not nearly so many of the abstract works that had been planned for inclusion and which Kandinsky and his comrades-in-arms had hoped would achieve far-reaching success. Above all Kandinsky had to defend himself more than ever against assertions that his work was derived from Cubism. He wrote several letters to Dézarrios, as well as articles for various art journals, stressing the simultaneous appearance of Cubism and abstract art on the art scene. "My sources on the other hand are Cézanne's paintings and late Fauvism, particularly the work of Matisse."

However, Kandinsky was very fond of the Italian Futurists, and recommended the work of Enrico Prampolini for the Jeu de Paume exhibition. He was not interested in the fascist ideology that Filippo Tommaso Marinetti and the Futurists had been caught up in, but rather in common points of interest that had already fascinated the "Blaue Reiter" group in Munich.

In spite of his withdrawal from worldly affairs into his artistic preoccupations, Kandinsky nevertheless soon found himself again thrust into the whirlpool of political events. Old friends from Berlin told him about the removal of his paintings from German museums. As of 1937 Kandinsky, along with many other modern artists, was considered a "degenerate artist" in Germany. The war years brought many privations for the Kandinskys as well. Kandinsky refused to go abroad or even leave Paris, and stayed in Neuilly in spite of offers made by trusted friends. He was supported above all by Jeanne Bucher, a gallery owner who

Colourful Ensemble, 1938
Buntes Ensemble
Oil and gloss paint on canvas,
116 x 89 cm
Paris, Musée National d'Art Moderne,
Centre Georges Pompidou

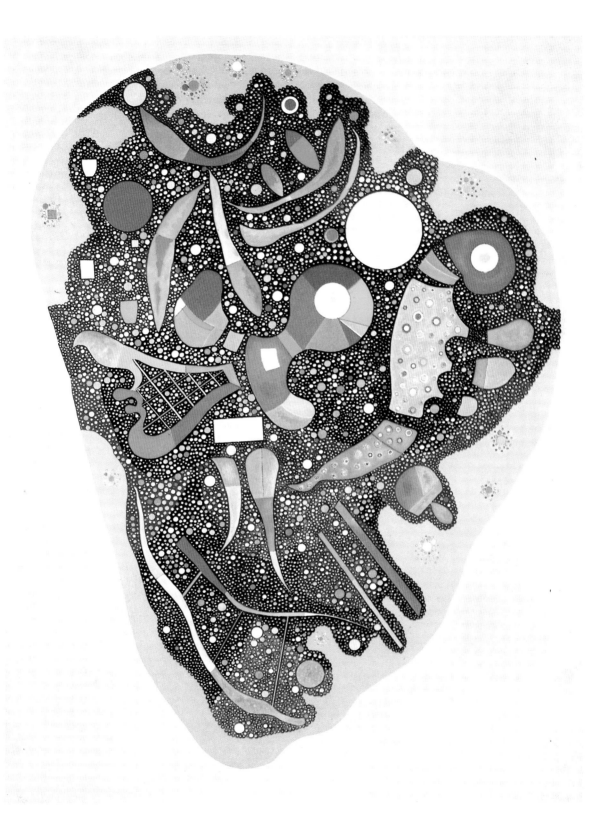

exhibited his work three times, even in 1942 under the difficult conditions of the German occupation. His later work in no way exhibits more of a sense of clarity or the wisdom of old age than his earlier work does. "Softened" geometrical forms and biomorphic derivations in shimmering colours animate the single-coloured surfaces. In *Around the Circle* (p. 89) the bizarre shapes of confined colours in a black pond glow like the domes of Moscow in the evening light. The composition around the red centre of the circle has a bewitching, fantastic, quasi-musical effect, as if Kandinsky had wanted to render the music of his compatriot, Stravinsky, in tones of colour. Until the very end, already restricted by the arteriosclerosis from which he died on 13 December 1944, Kandinsky continued painting on small pieces of cardboard. His last painting, *Tempered Elan* (p. 90) shows, aside from the tempered palette, as little of the external or internal threat as any of the other paintings from the war years.

Kandinsky was convinced of his "inner world" until the end. It was a visual world in which abstraction was not an end in itself or its use of form a "still-born" means of expression. It was meant to emerge from the desire for substance and life. Kandinsky's unique, expressive use of colour therefore owes more to the ro-

Composition X, 1939
Komposition X
Oil on canvas, 130 x 195 cm
Düsseldorf, Kunstsammlung
Nordrhein-Westfalen

mantic myth of creation, the emergence of new life from chaos, than to the flat geometry derived from a few basic forms that some Concretists and Constructivists tried to reduce his work to. Kandinsky was substantially involved in the most important undertakings in modern art. But above all he introduced a completely new conception of painting that he bequeathed to us in a variety of modes which were often received with hostility. It is a model of art that is non-representational, but understandable in substance. Very different artists and artistic trends have branched out from this model, followers of concrete, geometrical art as well as of gestural informality. But the resources of Kandinsky's ideas and theories have not yet been exhausted.

Around the Circle, 1940
Um den Kreis
Oil and enamel on canvas,
96.8 x 146 cm
New York, The Solomon
R. Guggenheim Museum

Tempered Elan, 1944
Gedämpfter Elan
Oil on cardboard, 42 x 58 cm
Paris, Musée National d'Art Moderne,
Centre Georges Pompidou

Untitled, 1941
Ohne Titel
Gouache, 48.1 x 31.2 cm
New York, The Solomon R. Guggenheim
Museum, The Hilla von Rebay
Foundation

Picture Analysis: Red Spot II

Kandinsky painted *Red Spot II* in 1921 at the end of his stay in Russia. This was a period in which his work was cool and balanced, after the surging chaos of colour and form of his years in Munich and the restlessness of his exile in Russia.

Within the confines of the painting there is a large, light base positioned at an angle, with its corners overlapping the edges. It is reminiscent of the Suprematist symbol, a single-coloured trapezoid, as it appeared particularly in the paintings of Malevich. But Kandinsky allows the edges of the painting to intersect this base in such a way that it is stretched into a rectangle. The free corners are filled out with cloud-like structures. On the upper left-hand side there are two floating lanceolate spots pierced through by white lances. The areas of penetration are marked out in black. The actual composition of the painting is situated on this dynamic, but solidly anchored surface. The "Red Spot" of the title forms the pulsating centre of the painting, and the other parts of the picture are grouped around it. A hook made up of several sections reaches round the spot and closes it in at the top. In the opposite direction two sharp horns press forward against the spot from the bottom. They are intersected by various curved and lanceolate shapes. A dark circle catches the larger, orange horn from behind. The use of the circle occurs here in some of its variations for the first time in Kandinsky's work. It became a dominant shape during his Bauhaus period. The circle was an important new symbol to Kandinsky in his basic analytical vocabulary. By varying the size and position of cir-

cles he creates an indefinable spatial structure, perhaps a representation of the mysterious "fourth dimension", the penetration of space and time that many modern artists, particularly the Cubists and Futurists, were striving for. The small shapes surrounded by a horseshoe curve directly next to the hook and the spot create a completely different sort of tension. In size and colour they produce a finer, more delicate effect in comparison to the main forms, like a gentle echo of the main theme. An irregular, yellow, four-sided figure mediates between the contrasting groups of large and small figures. A spatial tension arises from the penetration and overlapping of all the forms, a tension that keeps the entire composition in a state of suspended dynamism. Kandinsky experimented with the interrelations between primary colours and basic forms for the first time at INChUK, and suggestions of this can already be found in this piece. Alongside the tensions of surface and form there are also the tensions created by colour. While yellow is used more for the pointed shapes, red is reserved mainly for the solid, rounded-off spot. Nuances of blue are found only in the smaller forms and do not form any actual counterpoint.

Kandinsky had not yet fully realized the purity of colour that was to radiate from his "Bauhaus" work. But in this painting one notices the colours clarifying to a tone of pure contrasts – "Contrast and contradiction – that is our harmony", Kandinsky said about his sense of aesthetics. In fact, the effect produced by *Red Spot II* is not disharmonic, glaring or restless, in spite of the tensions between col-

ours and forms. The playful effect of the structure produces a calm, restful register of feeling similar to a symphonic chorus in which all the voices are tuned to one key: here, the strong major of the red spot. But seen together with the corners of the painting an impression is created of the cosmic, the elemental. Here Kandinsky draws nearer to the work of Malevich and Lissitsky, his Russian contemporaries, who were experimenting with a soaring, centrifugal arrangement of basic geometrical elements. What distinguishes Kandinsky's work from theirs is his unmistakable use of expressive colour and form, the wealth of interrelations, the characteristically eloquent, expressive style, the atmospheric use of space, and the imaginative use of ornamental, hieroglyphic forms, which reaches its full maturity in his late work. *Red Spot II* is an excellent example of Kandinsky's idea of "symphonic composition", "consisting of many forms subordinated to either a clearly defined or veiled main form. This main form can, on the face of it, be difficult to find, giving the inner basis a particularly strong tone. I call this complicated style of composition symphonic." The clearly subdivided construction of colour and form in this painting points to the next phase of Kandinsky's work, which began when he took up his teaching post at the "Bauhaus."

Red Spot II, 1921
Roter Fleck II
Oil on canvas, 131 x 181 cm
Munich, Städtische Galerie im
Lenbachhaus

Wassily Kandinsky: 1866–1944
A Chronology

1866 Kandinsky was born on 4 December, the son of a tea merchant in Moscow.

1871 The family moved to Odessa. Kandinsky's parents divorced. His aunt took over the task of bringing him up.

1876–1885 First drawing and music lessons; went to the classics grammar school in Odessa.

1886 Began studying law and economics at the University of Moscow.

1889 Commissioned by the "Society for Natural Science, Ethnography and Anthropology" to go on a research expedition to Vologda. The strong folk art of northern Russia made a lasting impression on him.

1892 Finished his studies and took his Law exams. Married his cousin Anya Chimiakin.

1893 Became lecturer at the University of Moscow. Wrote his dissertation on "The Legality of Workers' Wages".

1895 Worked as artistic director at Kucherev Printers in Moscow.

1896 Turned down an offer from the University of Tartu in order to devote

Kandinsky in Odessa, ca. 1871–1872

Kandinsky in Munich, 1897

himself to the study of painting. Moved to Munich and began his art studies at Azbè's art school.

1897 Met the painters Alexis von Jawlensky and Marianne von Werefkin at Azbè's. Went to the exhibition of the "Munich Sezession"; became preoccupied with Jugendstil (Art Nouveau).

1898 Applied unsuccessfully to study with Franz von Stuck at the Academy of Art. Continued independent work.

1900 Studied with Franz von Stuck at the Munich Academy of Art. Paul Klee studies with Stuck at the same time. In February Kandinsky showed his work at the exhibition of the "Moscow Artists Association".

1901 Together with Rolf Niczky, Waldemar Hecker, Gustav Freytag and Wilhelm Hüggen founded "Phalanx" an association for artists and the exhibition of their work. Elected president of the association. The "Phalanx School of Painting" opened in the winter under Kandinsky's directorship.

1902 Met Gabriele Münter, an art student. Second Phalanx exhibition. Exhibits with the Berlin "Sezession". Third Phalanx exhibition, including work by Lovis Corinth and Wilhelm Trübner. Spent part of the summer with his painting class in Kochel.

1903 Showed work by Claude Monet in the seventh "Phalanx exhibition." After the "Phalanx School of Painting" closed down, Kandinsky received an offer from Peter Behrens to teach a class on decorative painting at the Düsseldorf Academy of Art but turned it down.

1904 In the ninth "Phalanx exhibition" which was dedicated to Alfred Kubin, Kandinsky exhibited his own colour drawings and woodcuts. 15 of his works were exhibited by the "Moscow Artists Association". Worked on a theory of colour. He and his wife separated in September. Again travelled to many cities with Münter. His woodcut album "Poems Without Words" appeared in Moscow. Took part in the first exhibition at the "Salon d'Automne" in Paris, and again every year until 1910. In December the twelfth and last "Phalanx exhibition" took place.

1905 Took part in the exhibition of the "Moscow Artists Association". Became member of the German Artists Society. Exhibition at the Salon des Indépendants in Paris.

1906 Went to Paris with Münter and lived there till the end of the year. Showed his work in numerous exhibi-

Kandinsky in Dresden, 1905
Photo: Gabriele Münter

tions such as the "Salon d'Automne" in Paris, as well as in Dresden with the artists of "Die Brücke" and in Berlin with the "Sezession".

1907 Exhibited 109 works in the Musée du Peuple in Angers. Lived in Berlin with Münter from September 1907 till April 1908.

1908 Exhibition from March till May at "Salon des Indépendants" in Paris. Kandinsky, Münter, Jawlensky and Werefkin worked in Murnau from mid-August till the end of September.

1909 "Neue Künstlervereinigung München" (New Artists' Society of Munich) founded on 22 January. The first exhibition took place 1–15 December at the Moderne Galerie Thannhauser in Munich. Began work on "The Yellow Sound," a work for the theatre. Published "Xylographs" in Paris. Exhibited work at "Salon des Indépendants". First verre églomisé suggested by traditional Bavarian art. First "Improvisations".

1910 *Composition I.* Worked again in Murnau in February and March. Met Franz Marc during the second exhibition of the Society (1–14 Sept.) at Moderne Galerie Thannhauser. Stayed in Russia from 14 October till the end of the year. Exhibited 52 works at the "International Salon" in Odessa. Took part in "Karo Bube", an exhibition organized by Larionov.

1911 Corresponded with Schönberg. Resigned as president of New Artists' Society on 10 January. Involved with Marc and others in the publication "Im Kampf um die Kunst" (The Struggle for Art) as an answer to Carl Vinnen's pamphlet "Protest deutscher Künstler" (Protest of German Artists). First plans for "Der Blaue Reiter" almanac. On 2 December, during the preparations for the third Society exhibition, the jury rejected Kandinsky's *Composition V.* Kandinsky, Marc and Münter resigned. Divorced his wife. Opening of the first "Blaue Reiter" ex-

Maria and Franz Marc, Bernhard Koehler, Heinrich Campendonk, Thomas von Hartmann and Kandinsky in Ainmillerstrasse, Munich, 1911 Photo: Gabriele Münter

hibition at the Moderne Galerie Thannhauser on 18 December. "Concerning the Spiritual in Art" published by Piper.

1912 Second "Blaue Reiter" exhibition at the Galerie Hans Goltz in Munich (12 Feb.–April, graphic work only). "Der Blaue Reiter" almanac appeared in May. Kandinsky took part in numerous exhibitions. First individual exhibition at "Der Sturm" gallery in Berlin followed one in Rotterdam in November. Stayed in Russia from mid-October till mid-December. Took part in various exhibitions, including "Karo Bube" in Moscow and "Contemporary Painting" in Yekaterinodar.

1913 *Composition VI* and *Composition VII.* Exhibited in "Armory Show" in New York. First contact with Herwarth Walden. Kandinsky's essay "Painting as Pure Art" appeared in the journal "Der Sturm". His Reminiscences appeared in the album "Kandinsky 1901–1903". Took part in "Sturm" exhibition and the "First German Autumn Salon". "Klänge", his prose poems, were published by Piper.

1914 Individual exhibition at the Moderne Galerie Thannhauser in Munich and "Kreis für Kunst" in Cologne. Worked on four large paintings for Edwin A. Campbell's villa in New York. World War I broke out on 1 August. Fled to Switzerland with Münter on 3 August. Wrote "Violet Curtain", a work for the stage. Left Zürich on 25 November and travelled to Moscow via the Balkans. Settled in Moscow.

1915/1916 Last meeting with Münter in Stockholm during the winter.

1917 Married Nina Andreevsky, the daughter of a general, on 11 February. Honeymoon in Finnland. Birth of a son, Vsevdod, who died in 1920.

1918 Co-founder of a new model for the Russian art scene. Became member of the Moscow Artists' collegiate headed by Tatlin (this organization later became the Department of Fine Arts of the People's Commisariat – IZONARKOMPROS). Defended the principle of absolute art.

1919 In June became director of the Museum for Artistic Culture in Moscow, a post he held until January 1921. In November became chairman of the all-Russian commission for acquisitions for the museums of the Department of Fine Arts. Work by Kandinsky, Kasimir Malevich, El Lissitsky was exhibited along with work by other Russian artists in the First State Exhibition.

1920 Co-founder of INChUK (Institute for Artistic Culture). In autumn became head of the workshop at SUOMAS (State Art-Technical Workshops). Exhibition of 54 works in the XIX Exhibition of the All-Russian Central Exhibition Committee in Moscow. Increasing conflict with Rodchenko in autumn. Left INChUK and the Workshops for Monumental Painting at the beginning of 1921.

1921 Worked at RAChN, the Russian Academy of Aesthetics, headed the Department of Psychology, was elected vice-president. Headed the reproduction workshop. Returned to Germany in December 1921.

1922 Moved to Weimar in June and started work at the Bauhaus. Published a portfolio of graphic works entitled *Kleine Welten* (Small Worlds) at the Bauhaus in Weimar. Murals for the Unjuried Art Show in Berlin. His work was exhibited at "First Russian Art Exhibition" at the van Diemen Gallery in Berlin.

1923 First one-man exhibition in

Kandinsky in Munich, 1913 Photo: Martha Wolff

Wassily and Nina Kandinsky in Dessau, 1926

New York at the "Société Anonyme" (K. Dreier and M. Duchamp).

1924 Klee, Kandinsky, Jawlensky and Feininger the "Blaue Vier" (Blue Four) exhibits in USA.

1925 The Bauhaus moved to Dessau. The Kandinsky Society was founded.

1926 "Point and Line to Plane", Kandinsky's second important theoretical work, appeared in Munich. The first issue of the Bauhaus journal was dedicated to Kandinsky on his 60th birthday, and on this occasion retrospective exhibitions were organized

Kandinsky with his son Vsevdod in Moscow, 1918

in various German and other European cities.

1927 Taught class in free painting at the Bauhaus. In summer stayed with Schönberg and his wife at Wörth Lake in Austria.

1928 Became German citizen. Produced a work for stage to go with Mussorgsky's "Pictures at an Exhibition" at Friedrich Theater in Dessau.

1929 First one-man exhibition of watercolours and drawings at Galerie Zack in Paris.

1930 Travelled to Paris and Italy. Came into contact with "Cercle et Carré", group of artists, in Paris, and took part in their exhibition. The works of Kandinsky, Klee and Schlemmer were removed from the museum in Weimar by P. Schultze-Naumburg.

1932 The Bauhaus moved to Berlin.

1933 The Bauhaus closed down for good in July. Kandinsky moved to France at the end of December.

1934 Came into contact with the Abstraction-Création group. Exhibition at the Galerie des Cahiers d'Art. Met with Constantin Brancusi, Robert and Sonia Delaunay, Fernand Léger, Joan Miró, Piet Mondrian, Antoine Pevsner, Hans Arp and Alberto Magnelli.

1936 In the exhibitions "Abstract and Concrete" in London and "Cubism and Abstract Art" in New York.

1937 Kandinsky's work was shown in the Nazi exhibition of "Degenerate Art"; 57 of his pieces in German museums were confiscated.

1938 In the exhibition of abstract art at the Stedelijk Museum in Amsterdam. Wrote "Abstract or Concrete" for catalogue.

1939 Kandinsky and his wife became French citizens. Finished *Composition X*, his last major work.

1944 His last exhibition before his death took place at Galerie L'Esquisse in Paris. Kandinsky died of arteriosclerosis on 13 December in Neuilly-sur-Seine at the age of 78.

Kandinsky in Paris, 1935
Photo: Hannes Beckmann

The author and publishers wish to thank the following museums and collections for their support and loan of transparencies and photographic material (with page numbers of the illustrations): Berlin, Bauhaus-Archiv: 76; Berne, Kunstmuseum Bern: 74; Düsseldorf, Kunstsammlung Nordrhein-Westfalen: 73, 88; Frankfurt, Schirn Kunsthalle: 50, 52, 56; Cologne, Rheinisches Bildarchiv: 63; Munich, Städtische Galerie im Lenbachhaus: 2, 6, 8, 11, 12, 15, 16, 17, 19, 21, 22, 23, 25, 26, 27, 28, 29, 33, 34, 41, 45, 46, 47, 48, 53, 55, 67, 68, 69, 80, 93; Munich, Staatsgalerie moderner Kunst: 46; New York, The Museum of Modern Art: 31; New York, The Solomon R. Guggenheim Museum: 24, 43, 44, 49, 60, 64, 71, 72, 81, 89, 91; Photography: Myles Aronowitz: 24, 81; Photography: Carmelo Guadagno: 89; Photography: David Heald: 43, 44, 48, 60, 64, 71, 72, 84, 91; Paris, Musée National d'Art Moderne, Centre Georges Pompidou: 14, 36, 39, 43, 57, 59, 66, 75, 78, 83, 85, 87, 90; Peissenberg, Artothek: 46; Rotterdam, Museum Boymans-van Beuningen: 9, 32, 77; Stuttgart, Galerie Döbele: 70; further illustrations: The publisher's archives.